Called to Ministry, Now What!

§§

A foundational guide to your journey in ministry

PAULINE ADONGO

WESTBOW
PRESS®
A DIVISION OF THOMAS NELSON
& ZONDERVAN

WestBow Press books may be ordered through booksellers or by contacting:

WestBow Press
A Division of Thomas Nelson & Zondervan
1663 Liberty Drive
Bloomington, IN 47403
www.westbowpress.com
1 (866) 928-1240

ISBN: 978-1-5127-2760-9 (sc)
ISBN: 978-1-5127-2761-6 (e)

Library of Congress Control Number: 2016900876

Print information available on the last page.

WestBow Press rev. date: 1/22/2016

DEDICATION

§§

I am dedicating this book to my dear Mom, Kerina; who saw the calling in my life way before I did. Mom, thank you for the fervent prayers you have continually petitioned for me. Thank you for the ongoing spiritual, emotional and physical support you have provided me; a nurturing way beyond mothering. I love you. You are the best mother ever!

Also dedicating this book to Isaac and Miriam

FORWARD

§§

Our changing world has placed a very high demand on society and its spiritual leaders. The book, "Called to Ministry Now What; by Minister Pauline who is a woman of integrity, is an applicable tool in the hands of a Christian aspiring to become leader and desires to fulfill the call into ministry. By virtue of its content, this book shall enhance effectiveness and skills required to meet the demands and challenges that will arise. I highly recommend this timely book to you.

Apostle Joseph Atiemo
(Apostolic Empowerment and Revival Campaign, North Carolina. USA)

A call from God to a ministry is a high and heavenly calling which unfortunately, is taken lightly by some ministers today. Paul was called to be an apostle, preacher, and teacher unto the Gentiles and he never lost sight of his calling. He actively engaged in his ministry until his assignment was completed. Paul was first prayed for by a disciple called Ananias at Damascus. The most significant thing that Ananias did was to pray for the infilling of the Holy Spirit and for the removal of scales from Paul's eyes. In your call to ministry there is a need for scales to be removed from your eyes in order for you to understand the essence of your call. This comes through continued development.

There is big difference between training people and developing them. Training to some extent focuses on task, developing focuses on the person. We are called individually into a bigger vineyard that requires specific abilities and skills in fulfilling our assignment .This is stated in *I Corinthians 12:4-6*.*There are diversities of gifts, but the same Spirit. There are differences of ministries, but the same Lord. And there are diversities of activities, but it is the same God who works all in all."*

Pauline answers a profound question on the essence of the usage of our natural gifts in ministry hence breaking the invincible barriers between those that have the pulpit and those who work from the pews. Reading this book will steer you towards obtaining the right armor instead of trying to conform into someone's armor. David learned from King Saul but when the time came for him to follow his destiny, he could not have fought effectively wearing Saul's armor. This forced David to solely depend on God for the success of his appointment.

In your hands is a book written by a minister who has actually gone through the various stages and phases of development for ministry. This book is a blueprint for developing and maintaining ones focus not only for individuals entering ministry but more so for those who are already in ministry. "Hellen Keller said the only thing worse in having no sight is to have sight but no vision". Pauline Adongo challenges us to look beyond the physical drawbacks associated to ones call to ministry and instead depend solely on the direction of God and the partnership of the Holy Spirit in fulfilling our vision for the ministry.

Prophet Richard Owusu
(Senior Pastor Gethsemane Ministry Inc, Pennsylvania. USA)

ACKNOWLEDGEMENT

§§

I would like to thank ALL who have continued to support me in this journey. First, glorifying and thanking God, who has called and also provided the coaching and training of the Holy Spirit. This true Counsel who continues to lead and mentor me in immensurable ways, often leaving me in utter awe, bringing a totally different meaning to the word "awesome" in reference to God. Thank you Holy Spirit.

I acknowledge the Shepherds who first discerned the calling in me and were receptive by embracing, supporting and mentoring me in this journey. My sincere appreciation to Prophet Richard Owusu and Pastor Emmanuel Amoah of Gethsemane Ministries Inc., Sharon Hill, PA for stirring up what was in me and literally pulling it out!

Sincere thanks to Pastor Steve Sarago of East Gate Church, West Chester, PA. Thank you so much Pastor Steve for welcoming me with open arms. It's your nurturing big heart which embraces with sincere and true desire to bring the best out of us that remains admirable. There is such a freedom working with you and it makes a big difference.

To my siblings, Borna, Jose and Udi; nephews and nieces, thanks for your ongoing encouragement and supportive words. Each of you has contributed uniquely and individually to my life. I love and appreciate you all. To Bekki; "Whiteleaves". Hope to publish your columns and poems soon!

PREFACE

§§

To the Predestined and Chosen:

I have come to learn that gifts and talents are not limited to spiritual use only but are actually given to us by God for service back unto Him in all areas of life. I am a strong believer that "ministry is not limited to the pulpit, therefore each gift and talent should be applied as ministry in all settings including; business, corporate, academia, church, private and public sectors; as assignments from God to exemplify Him and provide the services as unto God with the ultimate goal that whatever we do brings glory to God.

This book has been written from a mentee's, student perspective. Though tailored to ministry, information provided in this book can be applied to any area of life, having the Word of God and the Holy Spirit as key mentors. However, since the focus of the book is ministry, the sole purpose for writing this book is to provide guidance to anyone who knows or senses that they have been called and chosen by the Lord, but lack direction on how to go about fulfilling their calling.

When God calls or appoints, He also provides the necessary resources to accomplish the assignment. This book serves as a foundational guide to those called and how to develop what God has placed in them.

Please note that I am still on the journey and believe that mentorship and training in the things of God are lifelong processes that we will go through until we go to heaven. I will attest like Apostle Paul in his letter to the Philippians that I have not attained, but I Pauline, I am pressing on, that I may lay hold of that which Christ Jesus has laid before me. This pressing on is a continuous process and I believe learning more about the things and ways of God is part of the "pressing on".

Ultimately, God brings the increase to the seed that has been sown in the form of a gift, talent or calling. I Corinthians 3: 6-7. God also provides means of watering the seed to fullness. It is my prayer that this book will stir up the seed in you to germinate while the Holy Spirit waters your seed to the increase that which God desires.

With weapons of righteousness in our right and left hands, let us fight the good fight of faith. Let's us run the race with endurance, being confident that He who chose us has begun a new work in us and He will bring it to completion until the day of Jesus Christ.

Pauline

TABLE OF CONTENTS

§§

§

BOOK-1
THE JOURNEY BEGINS

§

INTRODUCTION TO MINISTRY

§§

Scripture: - Before I formed you in the womb I knew you. Before you were born I set you apart; I appointed you as prophet to the nations. **Jeremiah 1:5**

"The seed in you determines what influences you", quoting Apostle Joseph Atiemo. In retrospect, as I reflect on my life, I was drawn to the things of God at a much earlier age but did not know that God was drawing me to Himself. From age 7, I always sensed a deeper desire for spirituality. Most of the time I could gaze at the clouds and picture God to be present, appearing dressed in white clothes. Though not born again, nor saved at that age, I frequently prayed at bedtime, and attended the closest church, always being drawn to spiritual things but not understanding why. I recall when I was 11 years old during the school breaks, I could spend time singing hymns and choruses and suddenly the atmosphere would change sending me in tears but I had no clue what was going on!

At age 12, I got saved and accepted Christ as my personal Savior. From there, the experiences got even more unique. Fortunately, I had a very good Shepherd then, Bishop Jonah Bedan, who taught us very well on the foundations after salvation and more so on the gifts of the Holy Spirit. Shortly after getting saved, night time prayer was mandated in our house. To side track, my entire family, Mom, two sisters and one brother all got saved on the same night in 1983, Hallelujah!

Shortly after we were baptized and filled with the Holy Ghost in the same house on a Saturday evening. The gifts of the Holy Spirit became more active in my brother Eliud and myself. My mother accounts to the operations of these gifts in both of us more vividly than Eliud. I recall because I believe both of us were young and had childlike faith so the supernatural were not unusual to us. I believe to us, these were common day to day experiences and not a big deal. Eliud for example frequently sang with angels and would wake up the next morning and teach everyone songs that were played in heaven. He was only 6 years old at that time. Eliud also had a prophet gift of hearing the voice of God and translating what the Holy Spirit had instructed. The gift in Eliud was and remains so powerful that he could stop the then Pastor Jonah Bedan while preaching and tell the Pastor Jonah what the Holy Spirit instructed. Pastor Johan also recognized this gift in Eliud and would stop right away and give Eliud the platform to speak! Now that I think of it, Pastor Jonah's actions were so humbling. He recognized the gift of the Holy Spirit and did not object to a 6 year old prophesying as long as he was the vessel God had chosen to speak through.

§ *Stay alert and open minded to the ways of the Lord and how He operates and speaks. God can use anything and anybody to relay His message or do His work; including the unsaved, homeless person and even a child to do His work. Do not despise or judge. Stay open to whom and what God will use*§

I experienced heavenly encounters mostly being at the throne of God and ministering to God in songs of worship with a host of angels. Throughout my teens, the key gifts that operated in me were singing, dreams and visions. I always prayed and interceded for people but thought all these were part of the package of salvation. Reading the Bible often consumed me. I recall while still in elementary school through high school how I could seclude myself and just indulge in reading the Bible back to back, sometimes reading from Genesis to Revelation, while at other times just focusing on the New Testament. It was during this period, I believe around age 16 or 17 that while reading a non-fiction novel while laying on a small veranda that I heard a voice very strong and firm tell me to stop reading fiction novels. At that particular moment the desire for reading fiction novels disappeared, literally. I lost taste for novels and started reading books by Christian authors. Oh Mom had a collection of them, the majority being T.L Osborn and Kenneth E. Haggin books. So I started reading these and still I have a growing library of Christian books now.

The gifts and inner drawing of the Holy Spirit continued to operate in me throughout my twenties to present. Interestingly these gifts would still operate even when I thought to have been far away from fellowship in the Lord. There was a period in my life during which I had backslidden, lived a compromised life and was not so fully committed to the Christian life; and yet the gifts especially those of visions and dreams continued to operate. Again, still naïve in the things of God, I still thought that these were just common general packages that came with salvation, and thought nothing serious of them.

In May 2009, I rededicated my life to God and made a firm commitment, purposed to fully serve the Lord with my mind, heart, body and everything to God. I submitted, and still do to the Lordship of Jesus Christ and the help of the Holy Spirit. The details of my testimony about my journey to submitting to Christ are in my first book *The Alternative Plan*. Following the rededication, I spent a lot of time in prayer and in fasting. Prayer though remained and continues to remain my key focus in connecting with God. Looking back, it appeared to be an intense draw and thirst to prayer and once again reading the Bible. This period of intense hunger and draw to prayer, reading the Bible and studying various topics in Christian growth lasted for approximately nine months. It was during this period that the gifts of the Holy Spirit were activated again. In fact, it was so funny, the first time I resumed speaking in tongues, and I was so shocked! See, I had considered myself so gone. I thought the Holy Spirit had left! In April 2009, I was attending a professional seminar in Las Vegas and was in the Caesars Palace hotel room on my knees praying. I even recall the verse that I applied for prayer that day ; **Galatians 2:20-***I have been crucified with Christ; It is no longer I who live, but Christ lives in me; the life which now I live in the flesh I live by faith in the Son of God, who loved me and gave Himself for me.* So shortly in prayer, the tongues came up! I remember having an utter shock, seriously, I raised my head up and questioned, "You mean Holy Spirit, and You are still there?" No, He did not leave. The Holy Spirit was there all along and once I recommitted myself to Christ, the fellowship of and with the Holy Spirit became even more frequent.

For since the creation of the world His invisible attributes are clearly seen, being understood by the things that are made, even His eternal power and Godhead, so that they are without excuse. **Romans 1:20**

****

Pause for reflection

The reason for sharing the background information in this chapter is to allow you to reflect on your personal journey and identify possible hints that may steer you towards desiring to develop your gifts. Take my example from the above:

♦ Worship and singing hymns- I am a singer and I love cross cultural Christian music and instruments.
♦ Prayer- I love to pray, I am intercessor.
♦ Reading- You recall, I was directed to stop reading novels, now I enjoy reading the Bible and studying. This may reflect a teaching gift.
♦ Visions and dreams- For now these are the ways God has chosen to speak to me. The gifts of the Spirit of knowledge, and or revelation and or counsel.
♦ Hearing the Voice, being told to stop reading novels-I need to know the Voice of God, Obeying the Holy Spirit. The gift of the Spirit of Wisdom.

Now look back on your spiritual life. First identify the key spiritual things that you find yourself drawn to and come with such ease when you do them. Should you find yourself frequently enjoying, having no difficulty as though natural, enjoying and being fruitful with these gifts; you are most likely gifted by God in those areas and now you need the Holy Spirit as your Teacher and the guidance of mature teachers in the Spirit to help you develop your gifts and eventually support you towards the full potential of your destiny in the call or in ministry.

CAN NATURAL GIFTS BE USED IN MINISTRY

§§

Scripture:- *Then the Lord spoke to Moses saying, see I have called by name Bezalel the son of Uri, the son of Hur: of the tribe of Judah. And I have filled him with the Spirit of God, in wisdom, in understanding, in knowledge and in all manner of workmanship to design the artist works, to work in gold in silver in bronze. In cutting jewels for setting, in carving wood and to work in all manner of workmanship. And indeed, I have appointed with him Aholiab the son of Ahisamach of the tribe of Dan: and I have put wisdom in the hearts of all the gifted artisans, that they make all that I have commanded you.* **Exodus 31:1-6**

The answer to the question for this chapter is yes! Natural gifts are needed and should be used in ministry. Well I hope from reading the first chapter of this book, you have identified that I am actually sharing my personal journey to ministry. My reason for sharing my experiences in this book is to help someone understand what they may be going through and pursue the full potential of their destiny. However, I am also careful to warn that God does not use the same experiences to train His chosen!

Now back to the question; can natural gifts be used in ministry? Once again the answer is yes! *Every good and perfect gift is from above and comes down from the Father (God) with whom there no variations or turning:* **James 1:17.** God bestows every gift to us. He is the giver of all gifts whether spiritual or natural. I also believe that God is all inclusive when He calls. He wants and demands your "whole you" not just some parts of you. Therefore, in addition to the spiritual gifts you have, you natural gifts are also essential and are equally needed in ministry. This reminds me of the ministry of Jesus Christ. Included in His disciples was a physician, fishermen and tent makers. Even the Lord Himself learned a trade, He was a carpenter prior to starting His ministry.

If you study the disciples and even the apostles afterwards in the Book of Acts and in the rest of the New Testament, you will notice that their natural gifts were equally paramount in supporting the gospel at various levels. Luke for instance, was a doctor and supported Apostle Paul caring for him while sick. Luke also applied his attention to detail as a physician to chronically write the accounts of Jesus in the Book of Luke as well as the details in the accounts of Acts of the Apostles. Paul on the other hand used his law and linguistic knowledge to wedge some strong defense independently whenever he was brought before the courts. We also see Paul use his natural skill as a tent maker to earn a living while still spreading the gospel.

While still referencing the question, God grants us the natural gifts to accomplish His divine will in us. The gifts are part and parcel, granted to fulfill our life given destiny. Exodus 31:1-6 our key scripture confirms that God is the one who gives and anoints every natural gift. It is up to us to utilize those gifts and appropriate them accordingly as God originally designed them to be used. As we reference this scripture, we see that God gave Bezalel and Aholiab specific natural gifts to accomplish a spiritual assignment which was to build the Tabernacle. Likewise, the natural gifts that God has given us are to be utilized to bring glory to Him and support His will on earth in the various settings He has assigned us to serve in.

Ministry is not limited to the four walls in the church. Ministry is not limited to the pulpit! As I indicated in my dedication page, ministry is a call within church and more so now outside the church walls. I am deeply convinced and purposed that Ministry is a Lifestyle just like salvation is a lifestyle. That said, we are ministers inside the church and the workplace. We are ministers at the gas station and while shopping for groceries. We are ministers during family meetings and while watching football! That also means that every professional gift and or natural gift that we have must be utilized as ministry to the Most High God, to bring Glory to His name. *Therefore, whether you eat or drink, or whatever you do, do all to the glory of God. 1Corinthians 10:31.*

§ *Ministry is not limited to the pulpit! Ministry is a Lifestyle just like salvation is a lifestyle. Constantly, we must be equipped and ready*

> *to minister in any setting we are in. God is omnipresent, so is the*
> *Holy Spirit and so are angels. We are ministers on the go!* §

That said, it would be helpful to identify and explain how natural gifts can be applied in ministry practically today. I will share my personal experiences here again. During a choir rehearsal in high school at the age of 17, I recall giving a suggestion to the choir and out of the blue, everybody responded positively to the suggestion and the problem was solved on the spot. This outcome caught me completely off guard because I had just joined the choir and was among members who had been in the choir for three years. I remember thinking how weird that reaction was. After high school, I spent time in the village with my grandmother and later at home with my siblings and in both residences, homemaking and organization, cleaning and putting things in order were my tendencies. These tendencies continued in my adulthood and actually got a bit stringent later in life because of my preference for structure and orderliness in all that I did. Later in my career and in my personal life, I noticed that God had gifted me with the ability to see or spot problems, identify corrective measures and put those measures in place systematically to resolve the issues. I discovered that God has given me the gift to work very fast, I tend to get bored easily, I realized that He had blessed me with the ability to troubleshoot, multitask and organize events. Both in my career and family life, I often volunteered to provide guidance where needed or just take the initiative to solve problems without being asked. Again being naïve, I just thought that these abilities and skills were as a result of my academic and professional exposure merely accepting them as part of the package too. I seriously did not think then that these gifts were God given for His purpose and His will!

The following is how the natural gifts have played out so far in ministry. Shortly after being saved at the age of 12, I was asked to teach the Sunday school. As I transitioned in the professional career I held key positions that required training fellow employees across the USA as well as within local regions. In my current position I have to evaluate staff development needs that are required for multiple tiers of peers, then develop and administer the training to all employees. Some of the training has been used at key corporate seminars or shared nationally within the organization. In my initial mentorship in ministry, I was responsible for developing training material and providing training for candidates who desired water baptism. I was also responsible for training new believers. A year after conducting these training sessions, God provided a platform for me to preach. So God birthed the teaching gift in Sunday school, developed it in the career setting (natural) and is now perfecting the teaching gift in his designated platforms. Glory be to God!

I have continued to use the gifts of trouble shooting, organization, structure and putting things together. I thank God for His grace and guidance in the application of these gifts both in the natural and in ministry. The larger part of my profession involved solving problems and organizing systems to keep them running smoothly. I am so grateful to God because in the various careers, He always alerted me to issues, at times in the middle of the night. So, I made a habit of placing a writing pad on my night stand and would wake up to write the ideas down. God still does this on issues concerning ministry and career. But I will never forget that first night He woke me up in 2006 to write specific instructions about a difficult situation at work! I praise Him still. Anyway, fast forward to 2013 through 2015 when I was asked by mentor again to host speakers and organize conferences -something I had never done before! Again, I thank the Holy Spirit for His guidance, support and encouragement for successful outcomes in hosting and planning the conferences. He combined the academic, intellectual, professional and spiritual gifts and had them all work together. God worked so well on these in that when I shared that I had not done any of the tasks before; everybody was amazed because they thought I was an expert. Thank you again Holy Spirit! The Holy Spirit is the true counsel. He guides in everything, even the minute details. Here again, we see God using the natural gifts for edifying His Church.

I see the same skills and process applied in my family setting. I will attribute to those skills and abilities to the grace of God, and to being the first born in the family. What I have observed in my family is that each sibling is gifted uniquely for specific assignments. This plays out wonderfully in my family. Peace-making and mediation is left to my younger brother Joseph. Critical thinking and debating all options is a skill of another. Firm stance left for the other and of course there is Pauline. Mom generally just listens then when she has had enough she will tell us all- Enough! It took us a while to recognize these specific gifts, but all siblings agree in the physical, each would want Joseph on their side. I finally concluded that God knew we were the only ones fit for each other, capable of tolerating and handling each other. That is why each sibling is in this family. So here too, you see how God creates unique gifts in siblings for the viability of a family.

*****

Pause for reflection

Based on the above, can we establish that every good and perfect gift is from above and comes down from the Father, our God? Good! Then let's also agree to I Corinthians 10:31 *that whatever we do, do all to the glory of God.* Have the assurance that it is God who gives and anoints us with our gifts. I encourage you to evaluate your talents. The discovery of the natural gifts were again though the revelation of the Holy Spirit, mostly during sessions in personal prayer and through prophesies of respectable and trusted Shepherds. I have to admit, most of the revelation concerning the gifts came much later in my walk in Christ, very recent I must say. Using my experiences, let's compare each area for application in ministry:

- ◆ Offering a suggestion that was carried through by the choir- a leadership trait, conflict resolution;
- ◆ Ability to troubleshoot, put systems in place, establish order, organize and bring order-an administrative trait;
- ◆ Cleaning and organizing- Interior design, church design, creativity, originality;
- ◆ Acceptance/open-mindedness- ability to deal with people with different personalities

I believe there are more that can be added to the list above if you can relate to the above. But take time to evaluate your gifts, from babysitting, homemaker, information technology, your role in your family, in business, customer service, lawyer, policeman hairdressing, auto mechanic to physician nurse, or any trade or profession. What are your natural gifts? How has God utilized your gifts in ministry? If called in ministry be open and be prepared and know that God will utilize both your spiritual and natural gifts to fulfill His purposes through you.

THE JOURNEY BEGINS

§§

Scripture: - A man's heart plan his way, but the Lord directs his steps.
Proverbs 16:9

To some the journey to ministry may begin way early in their Christian walk, while to others like me, it came much later. This could be because of utter ignorance (not knowing) or it could be due to disobedience, or ignoring the guidance of the Holy Spirit. "The delay in following God's will can be due to being in the wrong placement or sin", quoting Pastor Adego Afande.

I have come to learn that the journey to ministry is in stages and is very long. A respected teacher of the Word whom I love so much, Derek Prince, warns that "ministry is a marathon not a sprint". I attest to this and agree fully with Apostle Paul, in **Philippians 3:12-** *not that I have already attained, or am already perfected; but I press on, that I may lay hold of that which Christ Jesus has also laid hold for me.* I'm convinced that the journey is ongoing until we go to heaven.

In addition to being an ongoing journey, ministry is an individual walk. God calls us individually not as a group. He selects then elects His own. He does not call us to ministry collectively as a fellowship or peers or church or group. Examples from the entire Bible are quiet many: After Adam, God chooses Noah, from the nations of Noah, He hand-picked Abraham who becomes a father of many nations which includes Jacob, out of Jacob God picked Joseph, fast forward to David, then Jesus, then Peter followed by Paul not forgetting John the Baptist! So you see the pattern of elective "pickings". So there is a separation and election. I can only say that one may experience an inner dissatisfaction with their spiritual life and you sense a deeper desire to draw to God independently. I have testimonies of others who say they had supernatural experiences with God in solitude and that was the beginning of their journey in ministry.

The start of the ministry journey may begin with God drawing your attention to him. I believe God started alerting me of the call in 2003. I recall driving east on West Chester Pike, I even recall the exact spot where I heard a thought stating " maybe I should leave work for ministry and establish a church in vacant field off West Chester pike" . Immediately, I brushed that thought very quickly responding that "still wanted to pursue the career ladder and enjoy the accolades of the corporate world. Later on between 2005 through 2006, I felt as though I had an inner drawing to church and desired to join prayers teams and occasionally read the Bible. In 2007, the desire shifted to listening to Christian teachings on CDs. I recall watching Christian TV most of the time; actually habitually tuning in to television purposely on Sundays from 7pm to 9pm.

In the fall of 2008, there was an incident of what I have come to learn was spiritual warfare. I believe God allowed this to happen to draw my attention to prayer and to know that I needed to run to His shelter but I reacted very religiously to it. So I continued to order teaching tapes from various preachers. Of all the teaching CDs, "Back to Basics" by Bishop TD Jakes resonated a lot with me because in it, the Bishop seemed to be reading my then backslidden life and encouraging me to get back with God. I strongly believe that had I repented and sought God as directed by Bishop, I may have avoided what happened next.

In April 2009, I found myself unexpectedly without a job. I had climbed the corporate ladder, but I had learned in 2003 but God had His plans. Hence the introductory Scripture of this chapter. Pauline may plan with her heart but God SHALL direct her paths. It was during this period of solitude that I experienced a much deeper draw and desire for the things of God. To me, God used this period to reveal Himself to me as well as expose "me to me"!

In order for my journey to begin, God allowed what I valued the most to slip out of my hands. He brought me to a place of total surrender where I could not rely on my intelligence, professional skills or natural abilities. From the place of total surrender, I had to lose the sense of false security, success and the false identity of the world. I had to renounce the deceptive spirit of independence; which made me think I was too independent to seek God's guidance for my life. My journey began with God bringing me back to Him in the best way He knew how! Reference my other book *The Alternative Plan* if interested in how God got my attention!

******

Pause for reflection

My experience reminds me of the story of the prodigal son in **Luke 15: 11-32**; although mine now translates to the prodigal daughter. Initially, I had the inheritance of my Father which He promised to give and preserve me in order to utilize and accomplish His purposes. But in my disobedience and rebellion, I refused to stay and enjoy the inheritance. So He allowed me to come to my senses and could only do this by bringing me to the point of total surrender.

Reflect of your Christian life now and evaluate and think through instances, experiences, and a sense of being drawn to God.

♦ Are you being separated? Do you tend to want to be alone seeking God or more interested in spiritual things?

♦ Are you having supernatural experiences such as encounters with Jesus, heavenly dreams and visons, angels of God visiting, heavenly transformations to hear or receive from God and or the Holy Spirit? Impartations of the Holy Spirit?

♦ Is God drawing your attention?

♦ Do you sense a unique desire to get closer to God in prayer or in any other spiritual gifts?

♦ Are you experiencing a greater or frequent operation of the gifts God has given you now more than ever before?

♦ Are you experiencing a "shaking" where everything seems to be going on unexpectedly? This could be because a) God wants your attention b) God is warning you about something 3) you are in spiritual warfare.

♦ Have you come to a point of total surrender?

Based on personal experience if your answer is yes to most of the above, most likely, you need to return to God and He is waiting to embrace you and set you on course!

THE SCHREDDING

§§

Scripture: - But as He who has called you is holy, you also be holy in ALL your conduct because it is written, "Be ye holy because I am holy". **1Peter 1:15-16**

Shredding (definition) experience, peeling on an onion, layer to layer sequentially, outer core them inner core. Does in His timing, others receptive time based on maturity where He has matured you too, gain understanding, later chapter (Pruning for fresher oil and new impartation and greater works.)

In this ongoing journey, I've learned and I am constantly reminded that God is very orderly and structured in His ways! There are no shortcuts to God's ways. His principles and ways are unchangeable and should only be followed as they are. The ways of the Lord are righteous, true and just and ARE! That said, when God calls us to fellowship, we must accept that the Holy One is calling and have to present ourselves undefiled to Him.

I have named this process of preparing for God shredding because it involved an initial process of unveiling the sin in my life. God initiated this process through the fellowship and gifts of the Holy Spirit. Since dreams and visions were among the primary ways God communicated with me; every night from June 2009 though I can't really put a date, the Holy Spirit would expose the areas that I needed to repent through dreams and visions. So the next day I would start devotion by repenting. During this period, the Holy Spirit also led me to take communion every time I prayed. So I would take communion after repenting and immediately the desire for that sin would just lift off. I mean a lot of unclean things were disclosed by the Holy Spirit. Some were even out of my own character! Frankly the answer for that just came as I was writing the previous sentence that the out of character sins were because of the ungodly soul ties or covenants I was in while living the backslidden life. Thank you Holy Spirit!

Anyway, God really desires total purity; He did not leave any area untouched. He exposed character issues too including complaining, critical and judgmental spirit, pride, unfaithfulness in church, lack of commitment and false commitment to Him, lateness for church, attending church out of religion not out of commitment and love for God, not loving God, bitterness, anger, unforgiveness, not loving myself; God exposed countless areas and continues to do so to date. I consider this "personal shredding".

Next the Lord would expose again through dreams areas of sin that my family needed to repent. So I would approach God by repenting on behalf of Mother and siblings. At times, the areas that were exposed were real bad, one that if God was not relenting and long-suffering surely His judgement would have been dire! I understood and still d how the magnitude and impact of the sin caused by one person in the family could in turn affect a whole household, city of nation. Examples are Jonah's resistance, causing a storm in the sea. Most vivid is the sin of Achan in **Joshua Chapter 7** where the entire family suffered the consequences of one man's actions; even innocent children died because of this. Whenever God highlighted generational or familial sins, occasionally I would call my Mother and together, we would ask for repentance and receive the redemption of the Blood. So I thank God for His unfailing love that endures forever; He chose to forgive, save and bless if I repented. I also perceive this as God's love extended to show that He desires total wholeness and all good. *Beloved I pray that you prosper in ALL things even as your soul prospers (3 John 1:2).* This is God looking at holistic interest, not only focusing individually on me, but also looking at me as a package in a sense that nothing should defile me and my family generationally. Let's call this "familial shredding".

Social cycles were the other areas God shredded. During this period, I lost numerous acquaintances. Some disappeared without explanation, others I lost contact with, others I realized I had nothing of interest in common with and the rest God would expose them in dreams and those were my signals to know to walk away from the friendship or relationship. The dreams were very clear, the Holy Spirit really showed me their characters and where their hearts were in relation to their friendship to me. Some dreams could even manifest the next day and I would just obey the signs. The confirmations came when I realized after some time that none of the friends called and inquired about me once I stopped fostering those relationships. To some, I had to just be firm and say "I no longer can relate with you in that capacity". I deleted a lot of phone numbers and discarded a lot of gifts that would remind me of soul ties or relationships. We have just discussed "social or relational shredding."

§ *God calls each of us independently. Just because you are called in this journey does not mean everyone is in the same journey. God may be calling them separately and shredding them different for totally different assignments!* §

The most intriguing part of shredding is when I had to even separate myself and let go of those in the faith; fellow sisters and brethren, believers. It took me a while to understand this; but I still obeyed as the Holy Spirit directed. Later, by the revelation of the Holy Spirit, I learned that just because I am on this journey does not mean everyone is on the same journey. God may be calling them separately and shredding them differently for totally different assignments! Consider, Abraham had to separate from Lot first then relocate to promise destiny. Joseph was separated by being sold into slavery, and Daniel had to be in captivity, David through wars and in hiding, Jesus Christ through humbling Himself to become flesh, Paul through a Damascus experience! God does not use the same roadmap for who He elects. The appointment, timing and mode of getting one to accomplish His assignments are unique and different. This is shredding off "familiarity and life's pleasures".

Secondly, I have also learned that spiritual growth varies from one believer to another. So God being that He is all knowing may separate you by allowing you to lose fellow believers. Lastly, I believe God separates us from saints to wean us from dependency. So that if He wants to develop your prayer life, He may allow for your relationship with the church mother or prayer partner to cease in order to allow the full teaching of the Holy Spirit in prayer. *But in a great house there are not only vessels of gold and silver, but also of wood and clay, some of honor and some of dishonor. Therefore, if anyone cleanses from the latter, he will be a vessel of honor, sanctified and useful for the Master, prepared for every good work* **2 Timothy 2:20-21.** How about we label this, "shredding of religious practices and associations".

Since God desires for wholeness and is complete in all He does, the next area that God shredded was my environment. God is all present (omnipresent) and where He dwells must stay holy. The shredding of my environment came mostly through the conviction of the Holy Spirit, an inner knowing of things that I needed to get rid of from my house. Some of the items I had to discard off were musical Cds, movies, tight fitting clothes, mini dresses, anything under conviction that I sensed was not appropriate in my dwelling. With time, I dedicated my home and declared it a sanctuary of the Most High God. Shortly after this, I had a revelation from the Holy Spirit of how important it was to preserve this sanctuary. That meant I had to rely on the Holy Spirit and to be very sensitive to who and what came into my home. Furthermore, this also transcended even to the types of television stations I tuned to and the types of movies I watched. With time I lost interest for television. To date when I watch TV, it is still limited to news and documentaries, sports and occasionally old or clean comedies. All these happened way earlier on my journey, but I did not understand why. I just obeyed the leading of the Holy Spirit. I have now come to understand spiritual warfare and the reasons behind the Spirit's directive to be careful of who and what comes in His sanctuary; my home.

With time I have come to realize the magnitude of the environmental purging especially in this age of modern fashion designs where the occult, witchcraft and demonic designs can be disguised in art, fashion and furniture designs. I am writing this book in 2015, have you noticed the increased on snake scales and other reptiles or animals in clothing, jewelry and even soft drinks? In studying spiritual warfare, I have also became prayerfully mindful of gifts and learned to pray over them before I bought them home or used them. My point is that when God demands for holiness, we have to rely on the Holy Spirit for guidance but we should never knowingly defile what God has designated holy, both His temple (mind, soul, body) and our environment. *A little yeast works through the whole who batch of dough, Galatians 5:6*

Most of the shredding was done through Spirit prompted season of ongoing prayer and fasting as led of the Holy Spirit. It was in prayer that God exposed areas that needed purging. I prayed three times a day over this period normally at dawn, mid-day and bedtime. I must add that taking the Holy Communion at each prayer session was very powerful. I experienced greater and faster breakthrough doing this. On the Holy Communion, I later studied and utilized a dated booklet by Pastor Gregory Dickow. The booklet provided a prayer guide that I utilized when taking communion and frequently the outlined scripture for the day would be consistent with what the Holy Spirit had already highlighted through dreams during devotions or through an inner knowing. Frequently, I also prayed anointing all rooms and furniture in my house. I believed then and still do in consecrating God's house which I have dedicated to Him. Following prayer, I would dedicate most of the time to reading the Bible, sandwiched by reading various teachings and or listening to teaching materials.

The shredding period served for separation as well as purging. *Thus you are to be holy to Me, for I the Lord am holy; and I set you apart from peoples to be Mine* **Leviticus 20:26**.

*****

Pause for reflection

As you reflect, do you feel as though the Holy Spirit is "on your back" about some things? This conviction may not necessarily come through visions or avenues but other means:

♦ Is there something or an area(s) in your life that the Holy Spirit has reminded you to repent of?

♦ Are there friends or associates that you no longer feel free being around with; at times even for no good reasons?

♦ Have you lost taste for certain pleasures or habits? Please note that these may not be sinful things, they could even be spiritual things that you just have lost interest in.

♦ Do you feel as though you need to relinquish duties in a department or career and move on? Caution; be sure to prayerfully submit this question to God and only move after clear direction of the Holy Spirit. Satan is the god of confusion; God will not instruct you to leave a job if shortly after you have no means of supporting yourself. Prayer, Faith and Wisdom must be applied concurrently.

- ◆ Do you yearn for His Word and for holiness?
- ◆ Do you tend to hear the same areas the Holy Spirit has convicted you in radio, music, preaching even from secular settings?
- ◆ Do you sense an absolute need to be in God's presence, increased worship and hunger for fellowship with God?

If you are "being shredded", I would encourage you to surrender to God, submit, repent and obey the instructions of the Holy Spirit because you are being shredded for greater works! *Then Joshua said to the people, consecrate yourself for tomorrow God will do wonders among you.* **Joshua 3:5**

COMMITING TO THE CALL

§§

Scripture:- But Daniel PURPOSED in his heart that he would not defile himself with the portion of the king's delicacies nor with wine which he drank; therefore he requested of the chief of the eunuchs that he might not defile himself **Daniel 1:8**

Although already predestined and elected to ministry, I believe the next step is a matter of choice. It is appointed out of a really calculated decision making. A decision and choice that is made from the heart, the mind, and the body. It is a conscious decision that one has to make with an understanding of the implications of the decision and the associated risks.

Often, I reference the scripture above having being very grateful for the revelation of this Scripture. I recall reading this verse during the day while sitting at my desk. I can even relive the experience. This was an illuminating revelation; I saw a cloud of white light at the corner of this desk, partially resting on it while I was seated with the Bible open to the Book of Daniel. This happened in mid- summer 2009. The moment I read this verse, I sensed an opening in my brain and the word that kept playing repeatedly was "purposed". I learned here that Daniel had a choice to make here, so he purposed and made up his mind not to defile himself. Daniel made a conscious decision to serve God.

Committing to the call in ministry involves taking a risk. There are various things that must be considered seriously in decision making. I believe the biggest risks are willing to give up everything, facing the consequences and strictly living by faith, and trusting God in all areas of our lives. In the previous chapter, I discussed shedding or basically dying and letting go. Committing may involve risking friendships and relationships. Risking families, careers and hobbies. Commitment may involve even risking life. See the example set by Esther. *Then Esther told them to reply to Mordecai…and so I will go the king which is against the law: and if I perish, I perish!* **Esther 4:16**

Commitment involves counting the cost, evaluating what it takes and following through to completion, with the help of the Holy Spirit. Jesus in His instructions to the disciples outlines the cost of being a disciple or the cost of ministry. *If anyone comes to Me and does not hate his father and mother, wife and children, brothers and sisters, yes, and his own life also, he cannot be My disciple. And whoever does not bear his cross and come after Me cannot be My disciple. For which of you, intending to build a tower, does not sit down first and count the cost, whether he has enough to finish it lest, after he has laid the foundation, and is not able to finish, all who see it begin to mock him, saying, 'This man began to build and was not able to finish'? Or what king, going to make war against another king, does not sit down first and consider whether he is able with ten thousand to meet him who comes against him with twenty thousand? Or else, while the other is still a great way off, he sends a delegation and asks conditions of peace. So likewise, whoever of you does not forsake all that he has cannot be My disciple. Count the Cost-Jesus* **Luke 14:26-34**

Commitment also involves serving out a pure heart; rightfully so because God sees the heart where the motives and the intentions are set. *I the Lord, search the heart, I test the mind, even to give everyman according to his ways; according to the fruits of his doings* **Jeremiah 17:10**.There are countless warnings throughout the Bible cautioning against serving the Lord with lips and not the heart. Jesus in **Matthew 15: 8-9** quotes the Prophet Isaiah in 29; 13, cautioning that the people draw near to me with their mouth and honor Me with their lips but heart if far from me. Commitment must be from the heart. A key requirement in our walk with God and service in ministry among others are to serve and commit to Him out of our hearts. *And now Israel what does the Lord your God require from you, but to fear the Lord your God, to walk in all His ways and to Love Him,* **to serve the Lord your God with all your heart and with all your soul.**

Commitment to God and to the call out of love the basis of our salvation and heritance in Christ is Love. For God so loved the world that He sent His Son. Love sacrificed His Son to redeem us. God is Love. It is impossible to serve God without love that is like saying we have a coffee shop that does not serve coffee! How absurd! *Whoever confesses the Jesus* *is the Son of God, God abides in him (in that person) and he (the person in God. And we have known and believed the love God has for us. God is love, and he who abides in love abides in God, and God in him **1John 4; 15-16**.* If Love is in us, then we must serve out of love. This forces us to look at everything and everyone through the eyes of love as we serve in ministry. Here, love lays our foundation in ministry.

The commitment to serve in love and out of love transcends to our relationship with God and through our character. The Lord describes this relationship in *John 14:23-24 if anyone loves Me, he will keep My Word, and my Father will love him, and We will come to him and make our home with him. He who does not love me, does not keep My Words, and the Word which you hear is not mine but the Fathers who sent me.* Commitment to love for character is outlined in the summary of the Ten Commandments that Jesus gave; *and you shall love the Lord your God with all your heart, with all your soul, with all your mind, and with all your strength. This is the first commandment. And the second, like it, is this: 'You shall love your neighbor as yourself. There is no other commandment greater than these **Mark 12:30-31***

§ Chose to serve God intentionally in truth (His Word) and purity (Holiness) without which none can please God. Salvation is an independent walk. We are chosen individually and we will be judged individually. §

My commitment to God came way before the realization that I was called into ministry. In the previous chapters I discussed my rededication to Christ, but I believe the initial decision to commit to God came during the "shredding period" where God was cleansing me of sin and delivering me from false beliefs and from self-works of the flesh. My commitment to God required a total paradigm shift from serving God out of intellect and works, to serving God out my heart. My commitment came at the point of total surrender where I made the decision to become a born again Christian, newly dedicated to God with a made up mind to serve God out of truth and sincerity. I made up my mind that I would not serve God or be Christian out of formality, familiarity nor as a routine. I chose to be accountable to God and to myself. In fact I recall standing at a bathroom mirror when I made the decision of accountability. It was at this point that I came to the realization that salvation is an independent walk, we are chosen individually and we will be judged individually. I decided to consciously serve God in truth and purity. I chose to serve God intentionally. From this point on, I found and walked in the true meaning of salvation and refused to view this walk as a group, instead remain accountable to myself and staying in truth. My mind set and attitude about salvation changed. For example I refused to go to church just as a formality; people go to church on Sundays so I will go or people will join this department in church so I will join or I'm will fast because my sister is and so I'm fasting as well !! To date, I still refuse such lies. I have purposed to serve the Lord out of a pure heart and in truth!

******

Pause for reflection

I have resolved that God is looking for serious sons and daughters. He is looking for those who are sick and tired of playing church. He is looking for those who are fed up with religion. He is looking for those who are tired and have been exhausted with "works" in church and in their own walk. He is looking for those with great hunger and are thirsty for Him. God is looking for those who have made up their minds for Him. Those who are sold out for Jesus and just want to serve God period! Take time to reflect on these:

- Have you purposed to serve God?
- Have you considered the risks and can you take the risks?
- What costs have you counted?
- What are your motives for serving God?
- Have you evaluated your intentions for accepting the call to ministry?
- Are you at the point of total surrender or have you even surrendered yet?
- In Christ I live, In Christ I die. Are you there yet? I am.

Be serious. Once you made up your decision, the journey ahead is interesting and unique like none other.

One last thought, while still in this journey, I have discovered that commitment is ongoing! It is never a onetime deal. God is progressive; as we are being transformed from one glory to another. Therefore we have to constantly rededicate ourselves to His plans and will in the process. I will discuss this in another chapter.

THE MINISTRY OF THE HOLY SPIRIT: THE PERSONAL TRAINER

§§

*Scripture: But the Helper; the Holy Spirit, whom the Father will send in my name, He will teach you ALL things and bring to your remembrance all things that I sent to you **John 14:26.***

I begin this chapter by thanking God for the Holy Spirit. There is no way I can live this life in Christ without the person of the Holy Spirit. I thank Jesus Christ for the assurance of this wonderful companionship, and for surely not leaving us comfortless but providing the perpetual Gift of the Holy Spirit who is not only with us but is also IN us. Thank you Jesus! Thank you Holy Ghost!

This Scripture is very true to the works of the Holy Spirit. The Holy Spirit is the spirit of God. He is the heart of God and He hears directly from God to disperse to us; this includes guiding us through the road map God has outlined to fulfill His purpose in us. I believe the separation that God does when He initially calls us is to allow for intimacy with Him through fellowship with Holy Spirit. Solitude allows for time just to be with the Lord. So embrace the time in solitude fellowship with the Holy Spirit.

Experience with the Holy Spirit on spiritual growth

I testify to the sole training and guidance of the Holy Spirit especially after I made a commitment to serve God fully. He became and continues to be my personal trainer. As my companion and guide, the Holy Spirit's training during the period of solitude varied. In addition to dreams and visions which I shared earlier, other modes the Holy Spirit used and continues to use include:

♦ Revelation during Prayer. Most revelations, directions and declarations came during sessions of prayer. This would happen while praying and came with an inner knowing that the Holy Spirit is speaking. Once you establish a relationship with the Holy Spirit you will get to know Him. The way the Spirit relates and speaks varies from one person to another; but I believe He relates and speaks in the most comfortable form one can understand. My experience with the Holy Spirit has been the changes in the atmosphere. What I see is a transparent pure sense of light and freshness followed by oral declarations which may vary in intensity, force, volume, or pace. Frankly there are so many ways the Spirit moves during prayer that I cannot clearly explain. Moreover, it is unlikely that He will relate to you in the same manner.

♦ Prompting To Study or Research a Topic. Whenever this happened He would even lead me to the author of book or ministry. When I visited the website, the material would be right there! I recall in two separate occasions while standing by a bookshelf that is located in the basement, I was looking through the titles of the books and boom heard an inner voice "pick that one". The book was on faith by Kenneth E. Haggin. The other book was on prayer and fasting by Derek Prince. Interestingly, these books had been on these bookshelves for over six years!

♦ Craving for Knowledge in a Particular Area or Topic. Whenever God wanted me to learn about something, I would experience an intense craving towards that topic. So I would research it, buy CDs, and thoroughly study that topic to the point of expertise. This remains the most prominent way Holy Spirit trains me. I first experienced this at the beginning of 2015. At the turn of the New Year, one of my resolutions was to see and know the voice of the Lord. One afternoon while in the office, a sister walked into my office with a book, stating that she bought the book from a visiting Bishop. Bewilderment overtook me as I discovered the title of the book, *"Visions, Dreams and Their Interpretation" by Bishop Charles Agyinasare.* The book was autographed, *"Pauline, may you see"* Amen! When led this way, most of the time it is because God could be preparing you for several reasons; 1) for personal deliverance, 2) preparation for fresh impartation or elevation to a new level 3) preparation to minister to someone else. Juliet and the book on hearing God.

§ *The secrets things of God are revealed to us through the Holy Spirit. No eye has seen, nor ear has heard, no mind has conceived what God has prepared for those who love Him; but God has revealed it to us by His Spirit.* **I Corinthians 2:9-10.** §

Experience with the Holy Spirit on Character Building

I have come to experience or learn that the Holy Spirit trains in layers. It is once again like peeling an onion, being trained in one area of maturity to the next. Whereas initially His trainings to me were specific to understanding spiritual principles. As time progresses the training is shifted to issues of personal character and the importance of cultivating the fruits of the Spirit. Though ongoing, there is also a period in which the Holy Spirit's training shifts to walking in His character. Mostly He would allow for something to happen then I can only assume, He would watch my reaction? And if I do not pass, the test would be repeated! Have you been there?

My toughest challenges were anger and impatience. The tests in these areas normally came after reading and studying on walking in the love of God or after a period of fasting or prayer. At times the tests in these areas came through people who were very close and dear to me like my mother or siblings. I recall reacting in anger towards one of my siblings and the reaction did not leave a testimony that would draw my sibling to close to Christ whatsoever. Do not get me wrong! I did not curse however my tone was harsh as I yelled in anger in such a way that I could literally feel the rage inside me boiling immensely. Sadly, I felt no remorse whatsoever. Later when I came back to my senses I questioned my ungodly reactions. Despite my sibling being out of line, wrong is wrong, PERIOD! I repented and moved on and exactly two weeks later a similar occurrence procured from exactly the same person! I received the first call in the morning from the sibling as I was driving to work. As I am visualizing myself back there now, so much so that I can even show you the very spot in which I was driving flashbacks began to reveal themselves to me from the previous unsettling encounter. It was then that I adamantly decided to make a better choice and withhold all responses until further prompting. Gathering my thoughts and strength as I listened to hear His voice, I was then able to regain all composure and succeed at the test in such a way that would yield responses appeasing to the Lord. Shortly after, the test presented itself again as, someone bluntly disrespected me at work, however I was conscious and in the Spirit enough to rid myself of the anger as I was delivered yet again!

Experience with the Holy Spirit on Spiritual Warfare and Personal Deliverance

Although I had been a Christian for a long time, there were aspects of Spiritual warfare that I had quite grasped. I had the weapons of prayer, faith, the Word of God, the Blood of Jesus and the Name of Jesus Christ however very little on spiritual warfare. The Holy Spirit was loving enough to guide me to understand the demonic. I now believe that one of the reasons God drew me back to prayer in 2009 was because I was under demonic attack in the form of witchcraft and I had no clue of what was going on. The wonderful thing about God as well is that He didn't care that I did not know, as long as I used the weapons He provided. When I did, He prevailed! Hallelujah!

Or in depth study and exposure to understanding the dimensions and principles of spiritual warfare, and prayer, the Holy Spirit guided me to a fellowship whose primary focus was just that. God works in mysterious ways and I can strongly attest to that. A new colleague had just joined our department at work. One day as I approached her to inquire about a church that hosted an all-night prayer meeting and she quickly responded, *"They meet every last Friday of the month, you can visit this upcoming Sunday and evaluate the fellowship. This is the address. See you on Sunday"*. That Sunday I went to the fellowship although she didn't appear. I began attending for two ongoing and delightful years! I believe the Holy Spirit directed me there to learn about spiritual warfare among other things.

In addition to being guided to learn from the fellowship, the Holy Spirit also supplemented the training privately, mostly by revelation while praying. For example one morning after devotion, I heard an inner voice say *"study the cobra spirit"*. It is during prayer that the Holy Spirit would reveal demonic operations controlling environments and now with the knowledge, I pray strategically with understanding and also with the Spirit.

Most exhilarating was God's love expressed in the desire to make me whole and preserve all that concerns me specifically that of my family. It was during these periods of private fellowship in prayer and fasting that the Holy Spirit kept exposing demonic operations that were attacking my family, some were generation, others an elder group During this season many exposures were made mainly through dreams and visions. The Spirit also made some revelations simultaneously exposed to my mom and siblings at times during the same week. I recall a period that when I believe the Holy Spirit wanted to draw out attention to a demonic issue. The issue manifested at least twice in a dream. Within a week, my sister called me with the same issue she saw in dream! Throughout that entire month, major generational demonic altars were utterly destroyed to ashes. *Behold I have given you authority to trample on serpents and scorpions and over all power of the enemy and nothing shall my any means hurt you.* **Luke 10:19.** Glory Hallelujah, we are free! Thank you Holy Spirit!

Experience with the Holy Spirit on evidence of the Gifts of the Spirit in Operation

God does not tell me when He is imparting me with other gifts of the Holy Spirit, I just find myself operating in them! The only thing I can put a finger on that is tangible is the shift of atmosphere as an inner knowing of the presence of God and of the Holy Spirit reveals itself. With time, I have become to stay alert knowing God will show up anytime, anywhere and I mean it; absolutely anywhere!

§ *Tarry with the revelation in prayer until the Spirit reveals an answer. Revelation may also come in stages. So it is important to persist in prayer and stay open to the counsel of the Holy Spirit at each stage until full meaning is attained.*§

Retracting, the gifts of the Holy Spirit manifest themselves unannounced. For me this happened when I was praying for someone or when the evidence of what was revealed happened in real life, playing out picture perfect. At times I knew what to do with what was revealed, while at other times I did not necessarily know how to respond so I wrote things down a lot and still do. The first step was to inquire from the Holy Spirit to provide direction. I have also come to realize the importance of tarrying with the revelation in prayer until the Spirit reveals an answer. I have also learned that revelation may also come in stages. So it is important to persist in prayer and stay open to the counsel of the Holy Spirit at each stage. Matters that I did not have breakthrough in, I sort of mentored who was able to respond with in depth revelation. I will address mentorship in the upcoming chapters.

A word of caution would be that you must let the Holy Spirit direct and assign you the mentor. In order to be assured of sincerely mentorship, the foundation of that mentor must be rooted in Christ Jesus, in the Word of God, In the Holy Spirit and in truth and righteousness… *And will give you shepherds according to My heart, who will feed you with knowledge and understanding **Jeremiah 3:15.*** To gauge these, examine the fruits of mentor. Are the fruits Christ like? We shall know them by their fruits read. *Beware of false prophets (teachers/mentor in any area), who come to you in sheep's clothing, but inwardly they are ravenous wolves. You will know them by their fruits. Do men gather grapes from thorn bushes or figs from thistles? Even so, every good tree bears good fruit, but a bad tree bears bad fruit. A good tree cannot bear bad fruit, nor can a bad tree bear good fruit. Every tree that does not bear good fruit is cut down and thrown into the fire. Therefore, by their fruits you will know them. **Matthew 7:15-20***

The fruits of the Spirit are love, joy, peace, longsuffering, kindness, goodness, faithfulness, gentleness, and self-control. Against such there is no law. Galatian 5:22-23

Other Roles of the Holy Spirit

Let me highlight other roles of the Holy Spirit in this section just to supplement your understanding of the other areas the Spirit utilizes to train. I will expand on the foundational scriptures; **John 14: 15-16**- *I will pray to the Father and He will give you another Helper and He may abide with you forever. The Spirit of truth whom the world cannot receive, because it neither sees Him nor knows Him, for He dwells with you and will be in you.* See also, **John 16; 13-14** *through the Truth of God's Word, the Holy Spirit tells you what He hears from God. The Holy Spirit never speaks on His own. Everything He communicates to us if from God the Father.*

♦ The Holy Spirit is our ever present Helper and Comforter. He is with us and in us. He abides with us forever. Therefore, He can teach at any time and we can inquire of Him at any time.

♦ The Holy Spirit is God's Spokesperson to us. He reveals God's truth, the Word of God to us He never speaks on His own, and the Holy Spirit tells you what He hears from God. Everything He communicates is from God the Father.

♦ The Holy Spirit is our Main Teacher. He teaches us the things of God. Additionally, He brings to remembrance the Word (s) of God to us.

♦ The Holy Spirit Guides us into all Truth- As the Spirit of Truth, the Holy Spirit guides believer into truth. When we submit to Him, He guides every area of our life both in ministry and daily living.

♦ The Holy Spirit is our guide not controller. We are responsible for following His guidance or disobeying, but He will not force us to do anything. We are responsible for our words and actions

♦ The Holy Spirit reveals the secrets of God to us. He reveals the wealth and riches in Christ, the benefits we have in Christ. *I **Corinthians** 2:9-10* *"No eye has seen, no ear has heard, no mind has conceived what God has prepared for those who love him"* **but God has revealed it to us by his Spirit.**

♦ The Holy Spirit helps us discern between what is true and what is not; what is wise and what is foolish; what is best and what is mediocre;

♦ The Holy Spirit helps in decision making of daily living through discernment whether making large or small decisions.

♦ It is only by the Holy Spirit that we can do anything in ministry. *This is the Word of the Lord to Zerubbabel: Not by might nor by power, but by My Spirit says the Lord of hosts* **Zechariah 4:6.** Therefore the power and gifts to minister, teach, or witness the gospel of Jesus Christ is of and granted by the Holy Spirit. *And you shall receive power when the*

Holy Ghost comes upon you and you shall be witnesses to Me (Jesus) in Jerusalem and in all Judea & Samaria, and to the end of the earth **Acts 1: 8.**

♦ Finally, Rivers of Living Waters steam from what I would term the fullness of the Holy Spirit. These rivers are the abundant results of the work of the Holy Spirit in us which also include the fruits of the Holy Spirit. *Jesus stood and cried out (shouted) if anyone thirsts let him come to Me (Jesus) and drink. And he who believes as the scripture says out of his heart shall come streams of living water* **John 7:37-38.**

In conclusion, based on personal experience so far, effective fellowship with and benefits of the Holy Spirit requires total surrender and constant submission to the Holy Spirit. To get the benefits of any personal trainer, you have to obey the instructions and stick to the plan. Warning, I will not compare the Holy Spirit to mere human, He is incomparable!

******

Pause for Reflection

Before moving forward with reflections, it is crucial that we establish that you are filled with the Holy Spirit evident by speaking in the language of the Spirit, also known as speaking in tongues. If you do not by faith, ask the Holy Spirit to fill you with the gift of tongues. Most advisable is to seek the help of the Holy Spirit of brothers or sisters that may pray and lay hands on you to be filled with the Holy Spirit. If you are already filled, that is great! Let's then reflect on the following questions:

♦ Evaluate your life for the areas of sin that the Holy Spirit has convicted you in or exposed; have you sincerely repented of these areas?
♦ What character issues do you sense the Holy Spirit may be bringing to your attention? Do you see patterns of your own reactions to issues that are not in love or Christ like?
♦ What directives have the Holy Spirit given you concerning your family, finances, siblings and the like?
♦ Have you surrendered fully to the Holy Spirit?
♦ Have committed everything you own or have to the Holy Spirit?

◆ Do you sense a spiritual hunger or craving towards, the Word of God, to study a topic, to pray, worship or fast?

◆ Have you been writing down or journaling what the Holy Spirit has shown or told you?

◆ Have you put into practice (applied) what the Holy Spirit told you?

§

BOOK- II
NOW THAT YOU KNOW

§

SEEK MENTORSHIP AT THE DIRECTION OF THE HOLY SPIRIT

§§

*Scripture-And will give you shepherds according to my heart, who will feed you with knowledge and understanding **Jeremiah 3:15.***

The Holy Spirit does much of the training and mentorship independently and in private. I heard a renowned minister say that transformation starts privately with God before being launched publically. This has been true in the path of ministry; God reveals a lot to me independently. So those who oversee us spiritually normally clarify or elaborate what God has already spoken. Since they oversee, God can also speak new things to us through them. The key point that I would reiterate here, is to deliberately set time and prioritize, prayer, devotion, reading His Word and submitting to the Holy Spirit. These are paramount in knowing the heart of God. Prayer is our way of communicating to God, without communication we cannot know or hear back from Him. I cannot emphasize enough the importance of prayer and may I add, a purposeful life of prayer in order to be successful in any stage of preparation and later in ministry!

Emphasizing again, that it is through prayer, commitment and fellowship with the Holy Spirit that He reveals and guides us to the next destination or appointment in ministry. With time while in solitude with the Holy Spirit, I developed a deep passion for two things. One was to build churches. These were specific to building physical structures for churches in rural Africa. I would watch church services on You-tube and see believers meeting in churches that were patched up with sheet metal and believers kneeling on bare hard un-cemented floors while on their knees praying. That brought me tears. The second deep passion was a passion to preach the Word to billions and bring many to salvation, deliverance, healing, restoration, and restitution. Shortly after, I started writing sermons as inspired by the Holy Spirit. So I wrote and just saved them. Keep reading, I am going somewhere with all this…

§ *Do not submit to any mentorship; seek the guidance of the Holy Spirit! Both Jesus and Apostle Paul warn us of false teachers in the end times. To accurately follow the direction of the Holy Spirit, it is importance that you know God's voice for yourself and not rely on others to speak for you. Cultivating hearing God starts first in prayer* §

I believe God orchestrated my mentorship in ministry, it was a set up! While inquiring about a place that held all night prayer meetings, I did not know that this fellowship would serve as my first place for mentorship. It is amazing that when I inquired, I was specific to the type of fellowship and actually joined with a totally different motive! My first experience was that the presence of God was actually there! The second thing was that "these believers can pray some warfare prayers I have never heard before". That same night at service, the Senior Pastor prophesied over my life and confirmed the call into ministry with depth and clarity. This Senior Pastor operates in the office of the prophet, which as you may know, prophets should bring, edification, clarification and guidance. When I got home that night many things that the Holy Spirit had shared with me in private began to make sense! So I decided to visit the fellowship a few more times; thinking I like the prayer aspect of the fellowship and maybe that is all I needed to know; however, more prophesies came forth regarding my call into ministry and after just three months of attending the fellowship, I approached the Prophet, Senior Pastor and inquired whether he would mentor me in ministry.

God is a God of order! It turns out that one of the Prophet's calling is to mentor and develop ministers! Here again the Holy Spirit was guiding my steps to where I needed to get supplemental training. So I took the initiative and submitted to the Prophet to mentor me as led by the Spirit. My submission also came with decisive commitment to learn and graduate with an A+. The point I want to draw here is that I sought the help. Though the Prophet knew I was called to ministry, I had to seek the mentorship, not the other way around. I believe one must have a strong desire to develop and not be forced or coerced to mentorship.

The next and most critical step is to submit to the mentor and to the Holy Spirit. Understand the mentor only supplements the training, you still have to pursue personal development independently but simultaneously in private with the Holy Ghost. I must emphasize the importance of submission to a God appointed mentor. First is because they are assigned to God for you, in my opinion disobeying them would be equivalent to disobeying God. Second, they are too mature in what they are mentoring you in so submit to the teacher; not the teacher submitting to the student. Lastly, don't waste anybody's time. If you cannot submit or are too smart for the mentor, just end the mentorship and save everybody's time.

The following is just my principle in life by the revelation of the Holy Spirit; you may be smarter than your mentor in other areas and you may even recognize that, but it is wisdom to humble yourself and focus on the area God wants you to be mentored in despite the deficiencies or weaknesses you may observe in your mentor. After all *God has chosen the foolish things of the world to put to shame the wise and God has chosen the weak things of the world to put to shame the things that are mighty.* **ICorithians1:27.** Most grandmothers of our era were uneducated, but boy did they have wisdom. So if grandma cautioned we listened; our academic degrees did not matter when grandma spoke. With time you may even operate strongly in your gifts than your mentor, but humble yourself! Granted with time you may surpass your mentor in some areas, but remember mentors are also seasoned and have more experience in other areas too. Strive to balance each other; respect your mentor and never ever expose your mentor's weaknesses or attempt to upstage or overshadow your mentor!

Humility and submission allows for freedom for more in the latter aspects of the mentorship relationship. So I approached my mentorship with an open mind just wanting to learn more. When my mentor, the Prophet shared insights, I referenced the Word of God; always writing questions on what I did not understand. I also knew that my assignment to the Prophet would be short; so I purposed to learn fast and asked a lot of questions. I express myself better in writing, so I would prepare questions in advance to present at any scheduled mentoring sessions with my mentor.

> § *Take every assignment seriously. Purpose to be the best during mentorship. There are times you may just need to close your eyes ignore the negatives around you and jut focus on the assignment and the ultimate goal of your mentorship.* §

There were multiple assignments that I was given and they ranged from preparing sermons based on topics given, reading material and providing feedback, developing teaching outlines, being a forerunner for the Prophet, leading intercessory prayers, securing holy communion, supporting various auxiliaries in the fellowship, administrative functions and ministerial assignments. I also learned a lot by observation. Naturally, learning by observation is one of my main means of learning. So I would watch, listen and write down questions on issues I did not understand for presentation to my mentor when we met. Stay as open minded as possible to all areas of mentorship or assignments. Additionally, take every assignment seriously. Commit to be the best during mentorship. There are times you may just need to close your eyes ignore the negatives around you and just focus on the assignment and the ultimate goal of your mentorship.

As you note in the paragraph above, my mentorship was generalized covering most areas of ministry. At the point of my submission to mentorship, I still had no specifics of the calling other than what the Holy Spirit had shown me in prayer through dreams or visions. I did not come to the prophet with "I am called to be a BLV can you mentor me in that?" The Prophet on the other hand knew the specifics of my calling. I believe the comprehensive training he provided was because he was preparing me for the specifics and was also testing me. Yes, a good mentor should test you!

Hint- Stay in contact with the Holy Spirit, He will tell you when you are being tested by your mentor! Purpose to constantly walk and stay in the Spirit.

******

Pause for Action

I hope you realized that in the latter chapters of the book, the "purpose of the pause for action" sections is for you to take action not to reflect. Inky opinion, the mentor's sole intention is to water the seeds in us while God ultimately gives the increase as noted in 1Corinthians 3:7. Since water is needed to mature the seed to fruitfulness, it is very critical that you seek God assigned, pure water would result in good fruit. The role of the Holy Spirit in assigning you a mentor is crucial:

- Seek a mentor at the direction of the Holy Spirit. However also the person should be mature in the office and calling you are being mentored in. Do not seek a novice!
- Review the objectives and curriculum of the mentorship program/ process. Be very clear of each other's expectation.
- Identify duration of the mentorship.
- Submit to the mentor.
- Purpose to complete all assignments with excellence.
- Stay open minded and flexible to the mentorship process.
- Be sure to still maintain your personal prayer, devotion, study and fasting privately and independently.
- Beware that mentorship only supplements! Continue to fervently do your part.

MENTOR –MENTEE RELATIONSHIP

§§

Scripture: *Render therefore to ALL their due: taxes to whom taxes are due, customs to whom customs, respect to whom respect is due, honor to whom honor is due* **Romans 13:7**...*Elders (pastors) who lead effectively are worthy or double honor especially those who work hard at preaching or teaching* **1Timothy 5:17**

Professional and ministerial boundaries must be set at the very start of the mentorship relationship. Ideally, I would go as far as recommending that performance expectations, dos and don'ts be signed by both parties; minimally by the mentee, and expectations reviewed and signed. I did not sign in my first mentorship assignment but I purposely and independently set unwritten boundaries during my tenure with my mentor. I highly recommend that boundaries be set with any mentor regardless of their title or position in church or in the market place. As long as you are under anyone as a mentee, boundaries must be set.

I emphasize the need for boundaries because of the integrity of the Body of Christ globally. I learned this from watching Pastor Benny Hinn's teaching on how an individual sin can impact the entire Body of Christ because, though we are many, we are one in Christ Jesus. If one suffers, we all do. Subsequently, if one sins, the entire body is affected. I am very firm on setting boundaries. Your mentor is not your friend and you should not interact with him/her causally. Neither should you take advantage of your mentorship relationship and think you can do whatever you want in the church or the assignment given or go overboard familiarity with your mentor.

Setting boundaries, respect and honor are important elements of this process, carefully, being mindful that you are dealing with servants of

God. I personally believe that once assured that you are under a true servant of God, you may suffer judgement for misuse, neglect, overuse or abuse of the servant. So stick to my boundaries even if the mentor were to lower their guard, I'd keep your guard up! That's my other life principle. On respect and honor, address them with the preferred name. Know when to apply the brakes in action and in speech. This also refers to mentorship within the home or family setting. If the father or husband or mother is the mentor, and let's assume he is also the pastor, then at home he can be called father or dad, but once in church, if he prefers being called Pastor BLV, that his title in church.

> § Do not become fully dependent on your mentor that is
> idolatry. Substituting your mentor for God. Put your trust in
> God. Look up to seek God independently. Do your part§

Respect others your mentor may assign you to work under and don't relate to them with the same expectations you have of your mentor. If you do so you are setting yourself up for disappointment. Everyone is different. Each person teaches and mentors differently. As I cautioned above, swallow your pride, humble yourself and submit, close your eyes and learn what you need to learn. Such assignments are normally short-term anyway, so why throw a fit if you know you are only there for a short time!

Accessibility is very crucial in any teaching relationship. It is important that you ensure you can reach your mentor. A good mentor will foster open or two-way communication where you can speak comfortably without reservations. However, as a mentee, I would encourage that you inquire from your mentor how he or she can be accessed. Some may prefer email, face to face, telephone and in this age text or video conferencing. Once the preferred mode is identified, set boundaries and foster open, frequent, and ongoing contact. Accessibility is important not only for learning but for obtaining feedback in evaluating progress and outlining future goals.

Respect families, marriages and the mentor's personal space. Being under a mentor is not a license for intrusion. It is important to stay within the boundaries of accessibility being mindful that the mentor has a life outside church. If possible, mentorship should occur during fellowship hours and as designated however be sure to be as professional as possible for integrity purposes. That said, honor the mentor's family, marriage and personal life by being mindful of the times you call; limit late night or early morning calls. Honor marriages by respecting the marital boundaries and uphold purity and integrity. Rest is important to mentors, be sensitive to their needs as well allowing them to rest. Do not become overwhelming and dependent in the mentor. Doing that is Idolatry. Instead put your trust in God, seek God for yourself!

Seek your mentor in order to learn more. Silence does not always mean that everything is fine. This applies to both parties, the mentor may assume the mentee if fine. The mentee's silence on the other hand may be a reflection that the mentee is struggling! So as a mentee, take the initiative to reach out to your mentor.

Show interest in the mentorship process. This applies to both parties too but again the ball doesn't stop with the mentee. Complete assigned tasks by the help of the Holy Spirit with excellence. Be dependable and reliable for scheduled meetings and assignments. Go above and beyond the expected. Be alert and awake in meetings. Prepare for meetings in advance; doing this creates opportunities for in-depth discussions with your mentor that aren't rushed. Most important, respect each other's time.

Beware of tests from your mentor. Most of these tests are intentionally given by your mentor to evaluate obedience, character and performance as a mentee. For example, a mentor may cancel three consecutive scheduled appointments with you while at the same time assigning you additional projects. Your eyes should be on alert when this happens. It is likely that the mentor is testing or grooming you for completing God's assignment with endurance.

Continued growth in most things, whether spiritual or natural areas from personal experience requires challenging oneself. So challenge yourself and challenge your mentor respectfully. A good mentor may challenge you to do something you have never done. If this happens, it is good sign that you are maturing. Go straight to the Holy Spirit for guidance, believe me, the Holy Spirit will direct you. Guard your loins and take the challenge. Iron (mentor) sharpens dull iron (mentee), ask questions. Whenever you are in the presence of the mentor, squeeze every amount of knowledge you can from him/her. Use every encounter with your mentor as a learning opportunity.

A good mentor will allow you time to be independent and mature while he/she watches from a distance. My mentor did this countless times! I believe this serves as a period of evaluation to gauge where you are and what more needs to be done. If this happens, count it joy, you are maturing. As time goes on in the mentorship process, use this time to practice what you have done, research, and dig deep. This would be the period to review the mentorship process as well. Write the questions that arise from your reviews for future presentation to your mentor. Use this time to spend extra hours in prayer, reading the Bible, meditating on God's Word and fellowshipping with the Holy Spirit. Mentorship should never replace these four areas in your journey in ministry. If you ever find yourself overly consumed in mentorship responsibilities and have no time for prayer, reading the Bible, meditating on the Word and continual fellowship with the Holy Spirit, then it's time to push the stop button!

****

Pause to Action

As shared before, the mentoring process is a place of watering, where you gain more knowledge. While in the process review the following:

♦ Are you meeting the objectives of the mentorship?
♦ What are you doing to advance or hinder the process?
♦ Are your questions being answered?
♦ Are you free with your mentor and have you poured out all concerns related to the mentorship process?
♦ Do you still have adequate time to spend alone in prayer and with the Holy Spirit?
♦ Are you maturing in this process, stagnant or unsure? If unsure or stagnant, you should review the expectations with your mentor, review the second bullet point above or ask the Holy Spirit if you are in the right placement?

- Have you challenged yourself in order to gain more from the mentorship experience?
- Have you completed assigned tasks and have you passed the "tests" (from the mentor)? By the way the mentor may not outright tell you whether you have passed or not. You can gauge passing by being promoted to greater tasks or assigned more challenging assignments. You can gauge failing the tests by possibly being told, or being assigned similar assignments. Frankly, I am unsure as to otherwise to be certain. Generally I am very blunt, I would be forthcoming and telling you that you are failing. Leave it to your mentor to direct you but also inquire about your performance. Remember that in mentorship, the student takes the lead and the initiative, not the teacher.

TRANSITIONING-ENDING THE MENTORSHIP RELATIONSHIP

§§

Scripture: To everything there is a season, a time for every purpose under heaven. **Ecclesiastes 3:1**

Most of the studies that I have done in Christian growth show that God is a progressive God. He lifts us from glory to glory. So I believe that He directs our paths to get the training and shifts us to the next stage in His timing. God's timing is always the best. I am reminded of the accounts of Apostle Paul shortly after being converted. In preparation for his ministry, Apostle Paul was first in solitude, then on the road from one region to another studying and seeking counsel before he launched out .So we can conclude that once appointed, God also directs us to where we can be trained. God also objects to where we cannot go. So God sets the timetable for mentorship and the key is to be alert and recognize when the time is up!

I have never valued the importance of knowing the voice of God; the Holy Spirit until I ventured into ministry. It is very crucial to know and to obey the voice of the Lord even when things are going well. This brings us to next point which is critically important; that as a mentee you must pray, seek and cultivate HEARING GOD FOR YOURSELF, not someone else hearing God for you.

It became quite apparent from the very start that my first mentorship assignment was completely different from my tenure as I began the short-term fellowship. The problem is, I did not know God's definition of short-term, but I was very certain it was short-term. Eighteen months into the mentorship, around August 2014, I sensed the beginning of the end and knew I would not be with the fellowship in 2015. Around October 2014, I was quite convinced, I should end the mentorship before Christmas 2014. I disobeyed and instead pushed off ending the mentorship until March 2015.I approached my mentor who objected ending the mentorship, but on the other hand I disobeyed the Spirit. Oh thank God for His mercies and love that endure forever. Surely, He does not judge us based on the measure of our sins. Mark you all awhile, God kept sending me dreams and visions with clear direction to end the mentorship and move on to the next assignment! He sent four dreams all with the same message! So in May 2015 I officially relinquished my duties in the fellowship and ended the mentorship. Do not wait for God to warn you four times about anything. This is why it is important that you know the voice of God for yourself. The greatest counsel is of the Holy Ghost.

I would recommend the following as a guideline to ending a mentorship relationship or relationship with any ministry or department you have been serving:

◆ Be sure with confirmation from the Holy Spirit and or from your mentor that your assignment is over.
◆ Review the terms and goals of the mentorship and ensure all objectives have been majorly met. The reason for doing this is because you may still need to develop or enhance knowledge in some areas, but frankly in ministry, acquiring knowledge is ongoing.
◆ Set time to meet with your mentor to review the mentorship objectives and discuss the transition plans.
◆ Give status updates of assignments or projects you were given. This way the mentor can reassign what requires follow up.
◆ Formally thank your mentor for the mentorship through face to face meeting or a formal letter. Preferably and highly recommended is a face to face meeting.
◆ Do not leave unexpectedly. If you must leave, give advance notice, preferably a month is adequate.
◆ Maintain professionalism and respect your communication and interaction in your final meetings. This is key even when you have differences in opinion. Agree to disagree respectfully.
◆ Provide constructive criticism. Do not slander your mentor, ministry or department even if you were wronged or you know their

weaknesses. I am reminded of the story of Noah and his two sons in **Genesis 9:18-27. Also read Proverbs 30:17**

♦ Leave open doors of communication. Do not burn your bridges; end your mentorship with mutual respect for each other. One of my personal principles in life is that the *"world is a circle and frankly nowadays the world is getting smaller and smaller, you just never know where you will bump into your mentor again".*

*****

Pause for Action

Transitions are difficult generally within and outside ministry. It is said that people remember words than actions; but I also believe to leave better than how you came. Among my life's principles is also to leave something or return all things borrowed in a better position than it was handed. In ministry and in relations to mentorship is to be at peace with everyone. I Thessalonians 5:15. Peace is incorporated in the breastplate of righteousness which we must wear by walking in faith and love. To fully walk in love, we must forgive.

♦ I would encourage you to evaluate your relationships with mentors or pastors, churches or fellowships you have sat under and see if you left grudgingly or freely.

♦ If you have unresolved matters or concerns, pray and with the leadership of the Holy Spirit meet with the mentors or pastors and resolve the differences. Before meeting with them, also evaluate your role in this and be ready to ask them for their forgiveness. Be accountable and take ownership of your role in this. *Confess therefore your sins to one another, and pray for one another, that you may be healed. James 5:16.* The healing here would be from the offense or hurt that was caused.

♦ Repent for premature departure if sense you did and seek the guidance of the Holy Spirit on what you should do next.

♦ Examine yourself, repent if you spoke ill of your previous mentors, pastors or ministries. Call or meet them for reconciliation if led by the Spirit to do so.

♦ Strive to create peace with everyone.

LESSONS LEARNED IN MY FIRST MENTORSHIP EXPERIENCE

§§

Scripture: *The beginning of wisdom is this: get wisdom. Though it cost you all you have, get understanding.* **Proverbs 4:7**. *To Him who is able to do abundantly above all that ask or think, according to the power that works in us, to Him be the glory in the church by Christ Jesus to all generations, forever and ever, Amen!* **Ephesians 3:20-21**.

As shared previously, I joined the fellowship where I was eventually first mentored with the sole purpose of attending their all-night prayer meetings. I sought mentorship to learn the dimensions of spiritual warfare, prayer and the prophetic gifts. The key aspects of this fellowship were prayer and deliverance; all I know from my initial visits to fellowship is that "the believers prayed some prayers I had never heard before!" With time through the mentoring process, I discovered that I needed in depth exposure and understanding in most spiritual areas. In summary this is what I learned:

- Prayer; the importance of an individualized prayer life with prayer as the driving force that sustains our spiritual life. Also the importance of engaging long stretches of prayer.
- Fasting; the importance of it and not just the act of fasting but purposed fasting and praying through scripture within the duration of the fasting period.
- Fasting and prayer as part of preparation for ministry and continuation in ministry.
- The dimensions of spiritual warfare and how to deal with them, through prayer, fasting and the Word of God.

- The importance of having a grounded foundation through prayer, fasting, reading the Word, hearing God and fellowship with the Holy Spirit, which is the lesson, stood out the most for me.
- Studying to show yourself approved. I credit my mentor for this, whenever he found something he thought I needed, he either gave me the book or directed me towards the right direction.
- The different dimensions of the supernatural, the good, heavenly and the satanic and what to do with either of them.
- What prophetic instructions are?
- The importance of humility and character in ministry; other profound lessons.

I consider the following as exceedingly abundant, because I did not plan to learn them, God allowed me to:

- Hospitality, hosting speakers and organizing conferences.
- Assuming secretarial, ministerial and administrative duties.
- Learning about internal operations of a church.
- Teaching new beginner classes and supporting water baptism initiatives.
- So many more. I hope you get the idea that I went in for mentorship in one or two areas but came out with so much more. Now that is just God!

Despite growing in church from age 12, I had the foundation of the Word of God in me as well as I knew the gift and operation of the Holy Spirit but I still needed to understand other areas of the spiritual life. That is why I encourage you to stay open minded. Test all things still but be open to learning from God and from the teachers God appoints to you.

I know you are curious as to where I am after I transitioned from the fellowship where I was first mentored. Well, God just led me to another fellowship and here again I am learning other dimensions in the spiritual life. I would say the former fellowship laid the foundation for what I am learning now; as orderly as God would be. I needed to be exposed first in order to gain a better grasp than what I am learning now in my current church. So help me Holy Spirit I pray.

Let me end this chapter by warning that mentorship is a lifelong process until the day you complete your divinely given assignment. If fully committed to God, the first and ongoing mentorship will be that of the Holy Spirit followed by the mentorship of man (males or females who are assigned Shepherds over us). Ministry is so relational that for success, the Body of Christ must work together in unity. Consider the accounts of the disciples and mostly the accounts believers who supported Apostle Paul in ministry. Even our Lord had the disciples and sisters in the Lord supporting His work on earth.

So stay open minded, teachable and crave wisdom, knowledge and understanding. Remember we receive in order to give. As you are being mentored at various stages in this walk, soon you too will be mentoring someone else. These are now our fruits from mentorship(s); mentees becoming mentors.

******

Pause for Action

♦ What lessons did you learn from your first or many mentorship experiences? Write them down.
♦ What are your future objectives in pursuing mentorship in ministry?
♦ Are you ready or are you comfortable with mentoring someone else?

§

BOOK- III
GUARD UP YOUR LOINS

§

PERSONAL RESPONSIBILITY

§§

Scripture: - *Study to show thyself approved unto God, a workman that needs not to be ashamed, rightly dividing the Word.* **2 Timothy 2:15**

Mentorship only supplements personal training of the Holy Spirit. Personally, I believe 99% of the training and preparation is done in private under one on one training with God through our Helper and Teacher, the Holy Spirit. Only 1% of the training is presumed by the mentor. The reason being I believe is that God desires that we experience Him independently first before we share that experience to others. Secondly, there are just certain things God wants to reveal to us alone. So we need to distinctly know His voice and ways. Collectively, all these lead us to knowing God for ourselves!

Knowing God independently requires a personal responsibility and commitment. There is a part that we must do ourselves and not overly depend on pastors or mentors. Just like student would be expected to study independently, personal responsibility is required in preparation for ministry. Before I move forward with what the responsibilities are, it is important to revisit questions from the Book-1on Commitment: *a) Have you purposed to serve God? b) Have you considered the risks and can you take the risks? c) What costs have you counted? d) What are your motives for serving God? e) Have you evaluated your intentions for accepting the call to ministry? f) Are you at the point of total surrender or have you even surrendered yet? g) In Christ I live, In Christ I die. Are you there yet?*

What are your intentions or motives for ministry? As shared earlier, God is looking for those who will serve Him out of a pure heart. The intentions and motives for ministry must be holy and righteous and of the Spirit not of the flesh. They must bring glory to God not worship man. Intensions must be God centered not man centered. Intentions and motives must be holy and solely appointed for God's glory. The Holy Spirit must steer and direct our intentions and motives for ministry, not man, materialism or flesh.

In addition to intentions, we must also evaluate the ultimate goal. What are we working towards? What is the main purpose of venturing into ministry? Personally I am driven by two goals: (1) that the harvest is surely plentiful and there are no laborers. So I have submitted to labor and garner the harvest, (2 (this is my main goal) That Christ, the bridegroom is coming for his bride within the Church and my role is to equip the Church for His coming, **Revelation 21**. Remember He is coming for a Church or bride without stain or wrinkle, a pure and holy church that is why our intentions must be pure and holy.

Now, let's examine what personal responsibility takes. The key areas based on personal experience in this journey is PRAYER and lots of it. Collectively, the life of a successful person desiring ministry or with confirmed call should diligently and INTENTIONALLY COMMIT to more prayer, reading the Bible, meditating on the Word, fasting and studying. *Proverbs 4:7-Wisdom is the principal thing. Therefore, get wisdom: and with all thy getting, get understanding.* Committing to these consistently, always in the Holy Spirit results in spiritual growth and maturity. It is from here that that the fullness of God comes alive and you start experiencing God on a personal level.

Personal responsibility also requires total submission to the leadership and counsel of the Holy Spirit. In this relationship and fellowship, we must learn to discern the move of the Holy Spirit, walk in obedience to Him, know His voice and follow His instructions and finally apply what He has taught or directed practically throughout our daily lives. Through experience, I have learned that the Holy Spirit is very personable and He is not limited to spiritual areas. The Holy Spirit wants relationships in all areas of our lives, natural, financial, physical, spiritual and emotional. He loves participating in day to day living, providing guidance and protection.

The Holy Spirit is THE TRUE TEACHER. Through this intimate fellowship with the Holy Spirit, the deeper things of God are revealed. *Call on me, and*

I will answer you and show you great and mighty things which you do not know. **Jeremiah 33:3**. My personal experience in the earlier parts of the journey was to pray more in the language of the Spirit also known as praying in tongues. By pressing through in praying in tongues, I experienced and continue to develop deeper dimensions of the Holy Spirit. It is from here too that I believe more impartations, deliverances and gifts are cultivated. I experienced spiritual transformations and growth by praying more in the Spirit. Now I believe gifts of the Holy Spirit are imparted during these periods as well. More evident to me were the various tongues of the Holy Spirit and prophesies and declarations that are made by the Holy Spirit.

As an intercessor, the other profound experience is the Holy Spirit led intercession. Where once submitted, the Holy Spirit takes over the intercessions and directs the prayers! I love this about the Holy Spirit. Nowadays, I no longer initiate my own prayers. I have come to simply surrender and after I honor God in the beginning of each prayer followed by repentance, *I simply say Holy Spirit, I submit to you, now take over and direct this prayer!* From there, I let the Holy Spirit lead the prayer and stop when He deems necessary. At times I have cut Him short in prayer because I did not give Him ample time. Whenever that happens, *I repent, saying Holy Spirit I am sorry for cutting you short, Lord please forgive me.* However, I must share that this is the most exciting part of intercession or prayer because it is effortless, there is no exhaustion because, and the Holy Spirit is the one doing the work! Oh how I love Him! For further studies on praying in tongues, I recommend *Tongues beyond the Upper Room* by Kenneth E, Haggin.

I'm yet to discover a particular pattern that God uses during these periods of personal training or development. One that I am quite sure about is that He trains or reveals Himself in layers and in seasons. He does not load it on all at once. Most importantly, He tests and ensured that you have matured and passed the test before He reveals the next new thing. From personal experience, most of the adversities and tests I went through forced me to seek God's face more in prayer and fasting. The tests constantly bought me to a place of total surrender to Him. To die totally to the flesh, intellect and shape my character to be Christ like. You see *God is Spirit and those who worship or serve Him must worship Him in Spirit and truth.* **John 4:24.** So the flesh must die totally, leaving our spirit to connect with the Holy Spirit. I will discuss some character shaping tests that I experienced in this journey in the next chapter.

******

Pause to Action

To reiterate, mentorship only supplement the full training of the Holy Spirit. Examine yourself, have you submitted totally to God? Are you ready to be trained by Him? If so:

♦ Have established set times to pray, read the Bible, study and meditate on the Word; at most twice a day.

♦ Have you graduated past the 5-minute prayer time? Do you cultivate praying longer in tongues?

♦ Have you journaled what the Holy Spirit tells you in devotion and after devotion?

♦ What does your atmosphere look like; is it cluttered with noise and compromising music, social media and the like?

♦ Is your mind clear and receptive to hear from God at any time? Are you staying pure, body, mind, spirit (emotions)?

♦ When the last time you set aside was time to fast and seek God? How frequent do you this?

REJECTION, OFFENSE AND MOCKERY

§§

Scripture: -*Endure hardship as a good soldier of our Lord Jesus Christ, V¹⁰ Therefore, I ensure all things for the sake of the elect that they may obtain the salvation which is in Christ Jesus with eternal glory.*

2 Timothy 2: 3

I have come to experience God as one who desires wholeness in all areas of our lives. *The scripture I desire that you prosper in all things just as your souls prospers* **(3John 1; 2)** *comes true in my journey.* God desires completeness and wholeness in all areas and is not just limited to spiritual training of the soul. As His vessels, His aim is to groom us to maturity and total dependence on Him and not in other things or people. Because He desires for pure vessels, He uses or allows tests on our character to mold and shape us into His fullness.

Derek Prince teaches that God looks for those whose character will stand the test of time. From personal experience, the shaping of our character brings us to a position of internal toughening, boldness and courage where we are no longer weak however strong, timid and being led by our feelings. Through the shaping and molding of our character, our mindset, attitudes, perceptions and even personality traits are changed. Our hearts get stronger and we spiritually mature through the various tests that we face during the training and preparation periods in ministry.

Rejection, offenses and mockery maybe used to test and to shape your character. God may allow these to happen repeatedly until He accomplishes the purpose He wanted us to achieve or learn. Rejection in ministry may come through not being recognized for your efforts, being excluded in certain projects or groups or minimally involved, not being included in various cycles within the ministry, intentionally being denied or delayed opportunities to minister and being bypassed for promotions despite your exceptional performance.

Offenses come in various ways; outright verbal insults, public or private humiliation, insubordination from those working with you in ministry, being ignored or not being heard, repeated tardiness when you call for meetings, lack of follow through by others, jealousy, hate or strife, personality conflicts and misunderstandings. Sadly, you may experience these in ministry or within a church. It is important though that you look out also for offenses outside the church or ministry.

Most offenses will come from those close to you such as family members, coworkers and friends. The most hurtful offenses came from members of my immediate family at home and from believers in the fellowship. Not forgetting, whether from family or fellowship, I owned up to my share in contributing to the offense, although it's highly likely that you can be offended without you having instigating a single thing. Jesus Christ is our prime example for that.

Now having gone through it, I have concluded that ministry first starts with those closest to us before we venture outside. My lessons were that God allowed offenses from the immediate family to occur because I first had to show Christ to them before I show Christ to a pulpit in church. I had to forgive my sibling first before launching out to forgive in a church. Coming to think of it, God is so smart or rather wise. Think of it, since He is the God who cares about everything that concerns us, God trains me in the private (to deal with my sibling) so that I can know how to react to the offense that may be projected from the ministry or from work. Ministry starts from where you are and with whom you have more intimate relationships with. The light has to shine privately before it is brought out to shine broadly to others. Though the focus of this verse is giving, I am reminded of it here if you could read it in this context; 1Timothy 5: 8. *But is anyone does not provide for his own household, he has denied the faith and is worse than an unbeliever.*

Mockery may also be used to shape your character, however, I must warn that this too can be done blatantly or in very subtle ways. Blatant mockery may be presented as questions regarding your decision to pursue ministry, negative inquiries about the ministry, fellowship or church you are attending, issues regarding your past may be brought up, from personal experience, the worst type being "front biting". I learned this term eighteen years ago from a powerful general in the Lord from Nigeria, Front biting is when the preacher decides to confront you and preach targeting you right from the pulpit. Ignore such and stay focused on the assignment.

Be encouraged when rejection, offenses and mockery are projected towards you to shape your character. I perceived these as God's love for at a difference measure. *Moreover, whom He loves He chastens to be vessel of better and greater use .***Hebrews 12:6 and Proverbs 3:12.** Jesus in His teachings also shares that of the branch from the Vine (which He is) that has to be pruned to produce more. *Every branch in me that does not bear fruit He takes away; and every branch that bears fruit, He prunes that it may bear more fruit* **John15:2.** Paul also teaches that in the house there are various vessels made of wood, clay, silver and gold, all that have to be tested by fire for the master's use. **2 Timothy 2:20-21** therefore stand that when all is tested by fire you are not burnt like shaft but as gold come out purified in character seven times ready for God's use! Amen.

Recently I was reminded through prophesy that Jesus Christ was not liked by His own people. In fact His own siblings mocked Him, **John: 7:3-5.** Later on our Lord Himself warns us of the persecutions we will face and encourages use to endure to the end **John 16:33.** So let us endure to the end. For the suffering are temporary but the outcome if glorious **Romans 8:18.** Let us endure patiently keeping our face focused on the main goal of our assignments Christ was rejected, offended and mocked (scripture). Yet He ensured all for our salvation, deliverance, healing, restoration and restitution. *So count it all joy when you fall into various trials, knowing that the testing of your faith produces patience. But let patience have its perfect work, that you may be perfect and complete, lacking nothing.* **James 1:2-4.**

Jesus in His teachings to the disciplines warned that we should not be naïve, to be wise as (being alert of the ways of satan, **Matthew 10:18.** Paul also admonishes us to be vigilant because satan looks for whom to devour. This is why the relationship with Holy Spirit becomes key and crucial because not all rejections, mockery and offenses are from God. We need to be discerning to recognize the tactics of satan and be aware of any tactics, agents, ways, situations and circumstances he will assign or use. I have come to realize that this walk in ministry requires us to be alert all the time; vigilant and ready with our offensive and defensive armors at all times twenty four hours a day, every second, every hour,every minute! Once called and elected or rather as once taught "once you make a commitment to be sold out for God, satan will not be happy, and he will attack!"

Therefore, Satan may send people to reject, mock and offend you. Be discerning enough to recognize his demons and confront them. As I moved on with ministry, I noticed that some of the tests on this subject were literally demonic assignments. This was an eye opener to the realms of the demonic and understanding their operation inside the confines of the church. By revelation, I also started paying attention to repeated patterns in these areas outside church; at work, social settings and within family settings. The predominant demon that I observed was the demon of jealousy, pride, control and manipulation. The jezebel spirit operating through both females and males. In addition to the jezebel spirit also watch out for the "victimization spirit". Arthur Burk has a very good article on this spirit. Offenses can be attracted to someone demonized with this spirit. The victimization spirit attracts negative experiences. Renounce and rebuke this spirit in the Name of Jesus. Be free!

On the demonic front, we put on the full armor of God, *Ephesians 6:10-18* and we dismantle and burn altars. We take authority over principalities and powers, through vigilant targeted prayers, through fastings, through decree of the Word, through walking in love, through forgiveness, ongoing forgiveness, through releasing the offender and severing soul ties. Through burning and scattering enemies and uprooting even that which is dug and declaring the Kingdom of the Most High God be established in that!

Also not, that rejection, offenses and mockery whether designed to shape our character or are demonically inspired are distractions. In my experience, if sent to shape my character, if I delay to identify the character flaw that I need to adjust by submitting to Christ and to the Holy Spirit, the delay will distract me from getting the new "thing" I should be receiving from God as a promotion towards the next level of God's appointment or assignment. I have learned that God does not just chasten for fun or for chastening sake. In my experience whenever God has chastened through rejection, mockery or offenses. Usually, He cleanses an area in my life, bringing forth deliverance and healing, inflicting the necessary breaking; all leading to more submission and hunger for Him and thus acquiring yet another promotion in spiritual growth and often spiritual impartation of something fresh, new powerful and unique from His thrown.

Demonic steered rejection, offenses and mockery are generally sent to distract us from focusing on our assignments. When we dwell on the offense and fail to recognize the spirit behind them, we let our guard down for more damage, we neglect or limit prayer and spiritual warfare, we tend to fight from the flesh on our own; a place of defeat instead of fight by His Spirit, in the Holy Spirit; a guaranteed place of victory. In a tiny but very impactful booklet, Brother Kenneth Copeland teaches that satan uses offenses for the main purpose of stealing the Word of God from you and removing the anointing that goes with the Word of God. Excerpts from *Turn your Hurts into Harvests* by Brother Copeland. If struggling with how to deal with offenses, I highly recommend this booklet. It is a very short read. I read this book while celebrating my birthday in Montreal, Canada, shortly after suffering a major offense from a fellow believer. The book brought such deliverance from that particular incident and revelation on the offense. All things work for good for sure (scripture). See I didn't pack the book, I took my Mom with me on this birthday vacation and she had the book. One Saturday afternoon while relaxing in the hotel room she just passed the book to me to read not knowing what I was going through. See how God orchestrated my deliverance in a totally different way! The ways of our God; that would be another sermon or book, so allow me to get back on track.

"Do not lose your anointing over an offense or offenses. They are sent by satan to rub us of the anointing and block the flow of the blessings of God, Brother Copeland". There comes a time that the offenses and mockeries become a nuisance. At that point, once confirmed by the Holy Spirit that they are, put a stop to them. I believe strongly that Jesus while on earth was not a push over and so neither are his children! The nonsense has to stop.

Approach the person respectfully and in love caution the person to stop; again in love. If they don't want a respectful approach, I would still relay my expectations then let God avenge you. Let God fight for your behalf, it is beautiful to watch this unfold! Not that I would rejoice over the fall of an enemy but I have seen God fight mightily on my behalf, resulting in me laying prostrate at His feet in worship and awe because He just fought for me in an exceeding way.

Lastly, do not allow rejection, offense and mockery force you out prematurely. Stay the course until you come to full maturity in the area of training or in the preparation phase of ministry. If you have to cry, cry. Please take time to accept the hurt and grieve, just do not linger in this stage. As an Apostle once taught me, if you have to cry, give yourself a good cry in private, get it all out. Then wipe your tears and get yourself together, off on track you are again. Press through and complete the assignment or mentorship. Our warfare now turns to Psalm 33. Endure like a good soldier. Apostle Paul encourages us to run the good race which has many runners but only one wins the crown. *For our light affliction which is but for a moment, is working for us a far more exceeding and eternal weight of glory. While we do not look at the things which are seen. For the things which are seen are temporary, but the things which are not seen are eternal,* **2 Corinthians 4:17-18**

******

Pause for Action

You may experience a lot that may or has already come your way in the form of adversity, offenses and obstacles. Some may be extremely painful. My experience that the people who hurt me either did not care or remember that they hurt me. In fact their common response was "you cannot be too sensitive, or I don't know why you are at heads with so and so, worse yet; was "get over it". Bravely, the following day, you still have to greet your offender, smile and stay in fellowship like nothing really happened. It takes God to bring you to this level:

♦ Learn to forgive "on spot". Forgive immediately. At times I even turned around and asked the offender to forgive me too; despite knowing I was not the wrong.

♦ Evaluate your life now and forgive all types of offence, rejection, mockery and any hurt from your childhood.

♦ Break the soul tie with the offender. As long as you can still remember the offense or pain inflicted and react to it, your soul is still tied to the offender or abuser. So break the soul tie by the Blood or Jesus and in the Name of Jesus.

♦ Forgive all the offense. Renounce denounce and release the offender. Repent of any part you may have played.

♦ Receive the new in filling of the Holy Spirit; the new oil.

♦ Walk with power and boldly in the new anointing. Pursue the assignment God assigned you. Keep your head way up! Fear not. The God who called you, your strength, your deliverer, the One who sends His battalion of defense to deliver you, is with you. ***Psalm 147:10-12.***

SEEK GOD NOT THE GIFT

§§

Scripture:-Seek ye first the kingdom of God and everything else shall be added unto you. **Matthew 6:33.**

While you continue in your personal time with God, it is crucial that you reflect on the initial reason of why you are in ministry. Doing this will keep you focused on the main purpose and goal of your assignment. The only way to obtain the fullness of God is to relate to God in total submission and relation. Just like it would be in any relationship, it is important to maintain communication and interaction with the person, God is no exception. Purpose to relate to God just as you would relate to a close friend. Aggressively, seek the Creator!

Moreover, God desires this close interaction with me. He is an omnipresent God, ever available waiting for our communion with Him. I received this revelation one evening at a stop light while driving from work one spring evening. This was a during a period of sweet lingering presence of God when the revelation came; that He is God who wants to speak to us all the time and that He really longs for His children to connect with Him at every moment, every second.

Cultivate dwelling in His presence; through the sweet fellowship of the Holy Spirit. If they abide in me and me in them, I will come and dine with them. **Revelation 3:20 and John 14:23.** Regardless of your nationality or cultural, most deep conversations, openness and discussions occur around the dinner table while eating. When we dine with God in prayer, through His Word, through meditation, through fasting; when we just sit and relax in His presence, God opens up to use and exposes the details of His plans for us as we too open up to Him in this beautiful communion. It is in this fellowship that God reveals the inner secrets and mysteries to you.

My reason for stressing the importance of seeking God independently is because sadly, we are in the era where many are imitating other ministers or ministries in their pursuit to be accepted or revered; losing the authenticity and their own identity in the process. Do not try to be like anyone else or covert another ministers' gift. God is the one who chose us, therefore, He is the one who knows the gifts you need to accomplish His assignment through you. *You did not choose Me, but I chose you and appointed you that you should go and bear fruit, and that your fruit should remain. That whatever you ask the Father in My name, He may give you.* **John 15:16.** Therefore, let God mold you and shape you into what He wants you to be. Do not lust after another person's gift, style of presentation or change your assignment and calling to be like theirs. We need to imitate only one person; Christ Jesus and let His imagine be reflected in our callings, gifts and all aspects of our lives.

To avoid this lie whose root I believe is fear of failure and fear of not being accepted which manifests as lust, self-centeredness and insecurity, ask God to fill you with every perfect gift that is essential and needed to function in and complete His assignment in you. I was there before. I used to lust and long for every spiritual gift. If a heard about the supernatural, I prayed and asked for that. If I heard about the seer and prophetic gift, I asked for those too. I wanted it all. Finally one night while I was about to pray; standing at my prayer area, I saw by revelation the foolishness of such prayers In themselves, there is really nothing wrong but I felt inadequate and unprepared if I did not have all these gifts. However, the question that was posed through revelation was that "isn't God the one who chose me? Therefore He knows the gifts I need to accomplish each assignment He has given me". So in my prayers that night, I repented for my covetousness and repented to be someone else and changed the prayer to "God equip me with the gifts that are necessary to accomplish your will and assignment in me. Lord equip me with the gifts to complete your assignment in wisdom, in understanding, in counsel, in knowledge in the fear of the Lord, in faith, in power and in glory, in the blood of Jesus, by the power of the Holy Spirit and in the name of Jesus. Let these gifts be all consuming in power and the authority of the Holy Spirit. Let these gifts overflow in great abundance. Let these gifts operate in the fullness of the Holy Spirit with greater works, signs and wonders brining glory only to God's name, Amen!

Shortly after praying this prayer, I received multiple impartations of various gifts of the Spirit. The truth is that I did not know I had received them. I learned of them as I was ministering to people, smack right in the middle of the ministration, the Holy Spirit takes over and wonders are happening! Glory to God. I sense an increase in the depths of the gifts and responding thank you Jesus. When overwhelmed, I say 'wow "repeatedly and once the ministration is completed, I lay prostrate before God! Seriously how can one react to God after such visitation! Lord I worship you. Lord Jesus, I thank you! Jehovah, I exalt you.

When you read the accounts of the prophets in the Old Testament, disciples and apostles in the New Testament, in all accounts from Genesis to Revelation, whomever God called and chose to speak or represent Him, God Himself equipped and directed that person's assignment. No matter what some may have viewed as delays, God still equipped and delivered His promise for the ultimate accomplishment of His purposes. Consider these accounts; Abraham equipped as a father of many nations. Noah equipped with the supply and directions to build the ark. Joseph, staged, protected and finally promoted for the purpose of saving the Israelites from being wiped out due to hunger. Moses, David, King Solomon, Joshua, Caleb, Deborah, Gideon and Daniel equipped with leadership skills to protect and preserve God's people.

The scripture that continues to encourage me to stay glued to God and seek His face and not the gifts is *Jeremiah;1:4-8- Then the word of the Lord came to me, saying: Before I formed you in the womb I knew you; before you were born I sanctified you; I ordained you a prophet to the nations. "Then said I: "Ah, Lord God! Behold, I cannot speak, for I am a youth. "But the Lord said to me: "Do not say, 'I am a youth, 'for you shall go to all to whom I send you, and whatever I command you, you shall speak. Do not be afraid of their faces.* Prophet Jeremiah, may have stopped after telling God, 'Lord I cannot speak", then proceeded to imitating how other prophets speak. Then realize too that Prophet Jeremiah decided to remind God of his (Jeremiah's) weaknesses, but God who calls us with the awareness of what we are since He created us, provides the Prophet tools and means to accomplish the assignment. God responds, *"I will tell you what to say and I will protect you!"*

Now consider the disciples and apostles in the New Testament; Joseph our Lord's earthy father is given instructions about Jesus and protective directions from harm when Herod was after Jesus at birth. God empowers Jesus by the Holy Spirit on the day Jesus was baptized by John to complete the ultimate assignment, dying for our salvation. Jesus in turn empowers the disciples and apostles with the Holy Spirit, who guides us in truth, power and fire to accomplish the great commission. When God appoints, there is guaranteed supply from His thrown, every gift necessary for you to accomplish the assignment He has called you too. Praise God Almighty, who has equipped us with every good gift to do His will, working in us what is pleasing in His sight through Jesus Christ, to whom be glory for ever and ever Amen! **Hebrews 13:21**

The quest to seek spiritual gifts has the potential of exposing you to deceptive demonic spirits. Satan roams around looking for whom to devour; 1Peter 5:8. That is why we should be alert, sober and walk in God's wisdom always. When we lust or covet another's gifts; which by the way lust (flesh) and coveting (jealousy) are already demonic, we place ourselves in opportunist positions for satan to invade with any deceptive spirit. Satan is counterfeit, he mimics very well what looks likes God. So satan can be extremely deceptive in mirroring what appears real but yet very demonic. When driven by the flesh, we open the doors for demonic spirits camouflaged as God's ready to create havoc. So seek God. Moreover as ministers, there is now a level of accountability that we must accept once we submit to God in service. To whom much is given, much is required **Luke 12:48.**Our actions or inactions not only affect us but impact the entire body of Christ to whom we are assigned. So if we allow demonic operation in us because of our selfish desires, the consequence of our actions will affect many. By the way, that is also Satan's strategy; to use one person to target or affect many. I credit this teaching to my mentor. This is why when satan attacks just one pastor, the impact is never limited to just the pastor. The entire church and Body of Christ is affected. The news is heard on television and on social media. Satan's plot is to Strike the shepherd and scatter the sheep. So do not entertain any of Satan's deception. Do not negotiate, and do not compromise. Instead, attack in prayer and with the Word of God.

Be reminded that once committed to God, we must also die to self. This means we must die to independence and depend on God in areas of our lives. It is no longer about us but what He wants accomplished in us. "Self, I, my and mine", but all be crucified in order for the fullness of Christ and of the Holy Spirit to dwell and walk with us. Hence the meaning of the scripture; *I have been crucified with Christ ; it is no longer I who live, but Christ lives in me and the life I now live in the flesh I live by faith in the Son of God, who loved me and gave Himself for me.* **Galatians 2:20.**

Seek God, not the gifts. When we seek God's kingdom first, with all our mind, with all our strength and with all our hearts; all other things including the gifts shall be and are added to us. We also know, that when we ask, God responds, when we seek Him, we find Him. We knock, He opens. When we ask, He gives, exceedingly abundantly above what we think or know. The overflow are His mysteries and secrets; the unseen and the unheard. Hallelujah to the Lamb of God!

******

Pause for Action

In this chapter I will recommend that you pause for reflection then act. Have you been seeking the gifts or seeking God? Repent and renew your spirit and intentions for serving God.

◆ Examine your intentions and practices for any areas that you have imitated or acted like someone else.
◆ What types of prayers have you asked God concerning your ministry or calling?
◆ Have you duplicated what someone else is doing in you or ministry?
◆ Do you find yourself ministering, talking and acting like a pastor or preacher you admire?
◆ Evaluate, renounce and end any covenant with any demonic spirit that you may have allowed to operate in you based on self-ambition. Ask the Holy Spirit to expose these spirits. They are likely to manifest as religious spirits. Command them out in the Name of Jesus. Ask to be filled with the Holy Spirit.

- ◆ Determine and purpose to seek God first. Ask God to equip you with the specific gifts you will need to accomplish the assignment God gave you.
- ◆ Seek God by deliberately setting time for prayer, reading the Bible, meditating on the Word of God, and applying what the Holy Spirit tells.
- ◆ Pursue knowing God for yourself.

§

BOOK-IV
RELAX AND ENJOY YOUR TIME WITH GOD

§

DO NOT RUSH OR FIGHT FOR THE PULPIT

§§

Scriptures: *He has made everything beautiful in its time. Also He put eternity in their hearts, except that no one can find out the work that God does from beginning to the end.* **Ecclesiastes 3:11-10**-*For I am the God, and there is no other; I am God and there is none like Me. Declaring the end from the beginning, and from ancient of times things that are not yet done, saying My counsel shall stand, and I will do all my pleasure.* **- Isaiah 46:9b**

The main issue that I had to contend with during this process was the spirit or restlessness and anxiety. Despite learning fast and having more inside to pour, God is the one who trains and He determines when to launch someone. After all, He sees the end from the beginning just as He says here in the book of Isaiah. When He called us, He has already predestined our assignments, locations, territories, platforms and pulpits. It is His assignment anyway, so He must direct the ways of the assignment. I recall a season in this journey that I was overly anxious. I was aware of the magnitude of the call and started worrying about how, and when and where. So one Sunday after returning from church around 1p.m. God admonished me outright. I am very sure of this instruction. I was standing in the dining area facing the mirror and I heard very clearly; *"Pauline, this is my assignment, I will do with it what I want and when I want to, so back off!"* Firm, stern and clearly as it can be! I did. I let go of the anxiety.

We must wait for God's appointed time to promote and elevate us. Promotion comes from the Lord not man. Neither does promotion come from the demonstration of gifts. **Psalm 75:6-7**. No matter how much we may feel ready and prepared to move, it is best to wait for God to promote and align the platform. Recently at a conference, a Prophetess warned me to be careful of people who would want to rush you because they see the gifts in you. Whenever this happens, do not be quick to accept the offers, instead seek God's guidance as to whether you need to take the assignment. Remember from the previous chapter, we have been crucified with Christ. Our lives are Christ's therefore He dictates and orders where we go and what platforms to minister in.

Throughout the Bible, God spent quite some years preparing the ones He called. So endure in the preparation and soak all God is training you in. I've come to agree with Apostle Paul when he says "*I have not attained or have I matured, but I press on that I may hold of that which Christ has laid hold for me*". *Philippians 3:12.* We will never fully attain the things of God until we go to heaven just like God continues to unleash and reveal new things day by day. Most of the time I stand gazed and amazed. The phrase "God you are amazing now has a totally different meaning. So stay utterly thirsty for God. Continue to learn, and learn as much as you can. When God sees the thirst, He fills it and in His timing, He will set you in action. It is then that God will make all things beautiful.

A second phase of anxiety came much later after about six months. This time though, I felt like I had something in me that I needed to release urgently to the world and this thing; actually it felt like a constant swirling fire in my chest. The pressure was so great, I told my pastor that it feels like I am about to burst. This feeling was later confirmed prophetically numerous times by various pastors and visiting speakers in church. God knowing my anxiety spoke through one of the visiting speakers too. He prayed for me saying "Lord help her relax and align her with the right people". Immediately, that anxiety lifted, and the pressure to burst and launch ceased. From there I started to experience what I can define as an exhilarating time with God and such inner peace. I experienced a calmness in my spirit and a lingering sweet transparent presence of God that stays with me.

So denounce any anxiety that would force you to want to launch out while unassigned by God. Remember if God Himself does not go with you, then you are launching out defenseless and in your power and flesh. You do this, failure is imminent! Recall the story of the Israelites going to war without inquiring of God and what happened; major defeat by their enemies (scripture). Recall the Israelites being guided by God in the desert, Cloud by day, fire glory at night, and the Israelites would shout "let

God arise and let His enemies be scattered! *Exodus 13:21-22. Exodus 14:19.* We need God's guidance! *In Zechariah 4:6 the Lord also warns, it is not by might...our own strength, nor by power...skills, abilities and gifts, but by the Spirit says the Lord.* The success in all of God's assignments are by and in the Spirit; under the control and direction of the Holy Spirit.

During this season of let's call it "built up pressure", you may be tempted to confront your mentors and assert yourself that your time is ready; now. Please do not do that. The mentors if assigned by God, also see and know the timing for your promotion. If your time is up and God has confirmed it, you will know and God will also work out your transition. Do not be anxious and do not launch out prematurely. Instead, continue to submit and wait patiently before the Lord and God will exalt you. I would advise that you "fuel" the pent up pressure by continuing to press more in prayer, studying the Bible and meditating on the Word of God. Use this time for more preparation.

By this time in your journey, I would hope you have identified what you are called for. If you have not, that will trigger more anxiety and you may find yourself fighting to get into so many things that are not necessarily your calling. If you are reading this chapter and are still not clear of your calling, this would be the best time to pray and ask for the guidance of the Holy Spirit. Secondly, you should return to your mentor and ask for clarity and finally, prayerfully consider that your season with the mentor maybe over and you need to move on to the next assigned mentor. I caution that this final step should be done prayerfully and if ending the mentorship relationship, do so respectfully. Also examine yourself, what have you contributed in failing to recognize your specific assignment! Could the problem be you? If so repent and yes, begin anew. The failure to recognize and walk in your assignment could lead to seeking other gifts and not God. A dangerous stance to take as discussed in the previous chapter.

If you know your assignment, continue to prepare and fine tune yourself. Study to make yourself approved *2 Timothy 2:15*.Get wisdom, but also get understanding *Proverbs 4:5-9*. If called to sing, study various music, take voice lessons. If called to minister through preaching, counseling, children's ministry and in any of the fivefold offices in ministry, continue to study and prepare yourself. Do all the preparation you can so that if called upon at any time, you can be prepared at your appointed time for the assignment.

Take every assignment you are given very seriously and prepare for it fully. Regardless of whether the assignment is, big or small, whether you feel it is mediocre or beyond your abilities. Prepare and take the assignment seriously. These assignments may be your launching pads as well as your testing grounds. The tests for commitment, character and attitude start with such types of assignments. If you are too anointed to take the trash out or arrange the chairs in church while still a mentee; you have just failed. If you are asked to teach six people and you are arguing with the pastor over teaching twenty five or preaching to the congregation, you have just failed. If you rather prophesy to people than intercede for them at the direction of your mentor, you have failed. I am pleading with you now, at this level of mentorship and training, if rebellion, pride and self are still evident, it is time you questioned your decision to be in ministry in the first place.

Through experience, I have come to embrace these assignments as they have taught me a great deal... From them I have been able to evaluate and get feedback in regards to my progress, strengths, and weakness... My mentors observe and give the appropriate feedback as to what I did well and what I should improve upon. You just never know. I am learning that God does not really tell you when He will launch you! One day, the worship leader fails to show up, others point at you to lead worship, boom, and you are launched. One Sunday morning, the pastor assigns you to teach adult Sunday school. The pastor comes in at 10 a.m. and tells you, "proceed with preaching today, what you taught at Sunday school earlier was very good". There you are, launched!

Finally, it is important to be officially prayed for, blessed, anointed and activated in your calling. This time too will be determined and orchestrated by God. David was anointed straight from the fields and he became king after quite some time. Before he stepped to rule, David was anointed again. I would caution against bypassing steps and self-promotion. King Saul was appointed by people. His end was disastrous. Absalom David's son coerced people against David his own father and failed in a very short-term tenure of rulership. The other lesson from Absalom's rebellion is the "self-appointed titles". Do not designate yourself a title until you have been commissioned! Do not force people to address you as apostle, prophet, minister, or whatever title of choice unless officially designated. Frankly, in reading the accounts of the disciples, I could not find any account of the disciples addressing each other with titles. The Spirit in His assignments to the church says, separate me Barnabas and Paul. Apostle Paul mostly uses his designation in the introductory parts of his letters to the church. In most of his letters, Paul address other disciples, his sons by first names and others by their careers, such as Luke the physician, Alexander the coppersmith. Rarely does Paul address his fellow apostles by titles. I must say, this fixation on titles within the Body of Christ is one of my pet peeves.

My mentor and I discussed this issue of self-promotion in ministry recently and the concept and I asked "*where are the fathers or mothers when modern preachers and prophets are acting out of order?*" My mentor responded, "Oh, they think they do not need the fathers and mothers any more". I still want to tell my mentor, "*the kids have outgrown their parents ah!' The sons and daughters are too mature than the shepherds who are mentoring them!* Satan I rebuke you in the name of Jesus! I rebuke this lie in the name of Jesus!

In God's timing He makes everything beautiful. At His appointed time, He will promote you beautifully. God will launch you at His appointed time. He will make all things beautiful by providing all you need for your assignment; the finances, committed helpers, instruments, divine connections, favor and grace to accomplish the task at hand. He sees the end from the beginning but He also plans for the in between. So, relax, wait upon the Lord by preparing, enhancing and maturing yourself with the help of the Holy Spirit. Then let God promote you.

******

Pause for Action

Casting all your anxieties to God for He cares for you! You should know this scripture by now. Cast everything to Him, your concerns and questions. I mean everything. Be blunt and sincere with God.

- ◆ Repent, renounce restlessness or anxiety and resubmit yourself to God if at all you have acted hastily in promoting yourself.
- ◆ Repent and meet with your mentors if at all you have disobeyed their instructions and launched independently of them.
- ◆ Repent and reconcile with your mentors if you have slandered or caused disruption in your mentor's gatherings on your way out to launch your ministry. This includes, taking your mentor's members with you or holding secret side gatherings with them.
- ◆ Ask God to show you the next steps, open His designated doors, connections and platforms. You may need to seek God through prayer and fastings on this.
- ◆ Ask God to continue to clarify the assignments He has designated for you. You may need to seek God through prayer and fastings on this.
- ◆ Continue to see God, not the gifts, not the platform, nor microphone. Seek God.

ENJOY YOUR SEASONS
WITH THE HOLY SPIRIT

§§

Scripture-_And it shall come to pass afterward, that I will pour out My Spirit on all flesh(mankind);your sons and your daughters shall prophesy, your old men shall dream dreams, your young men shall see visions. And also on My menservants and on My maidservants. I will pour out My Spirit in those days._
Joel: 28-29

I am going to base this chapter solely based on the personal experience I have in this journey. The previous chapters are majorly based on personal experience also but on this particular topic I would rather personalize it because God works differently with each one He calls. His methods are rarely the same.

Shortly after being delivered from the anxiety and building pressure of "when Lord when", I started experiencing the fullness of joy of the Holy Spirit. The presence of God and fellowship became more and more frequent to the point where I can boldly say a lifestyle. God's presence though sovereign is also very sweet. This reminds of the scriptures that says, He stays above as God but yet delights to commune with us. _For this is what The High and Exalted One says, He who lives forever, whose Name is holy; I live in a high and holy place,_ **but** _also with him who has a contrite and a humble spirit. To revive the spirit of the humble and to revive the heart of the contrite ones_ **Isaiah 57:15.**

God truly desires to abide with us. My experience is that He doesn't care where you will be when He is ready for fellowship. It could be in the car, at work, at the gas station and even in the restroom or shower. I had to quickly accept these experiences because He could just show up. Before these experiences, I had the preconceptions about how God interacts. I thought it only occurred during prayer; when we are presentable and "well behaved"! So the first time He spoke to me when I was closing the bathroom door, I went "oh, you mean you (God), you just show up like that; you don't care that I'm not presentable"? I renounced my preconceptions and His glory manifested and continues to do so frequently. I now live in and with the awareness of God's presence and submit to whatever He wants to do. This usually brings me to a place of total surrender. If driving, I will pull over, while at home, I will just let the Holy Spirit minister until He is finished. I've discovered that God may alter my schedules and plans as well, so I've learned to be flexible with the Holy Spirit. *Pauline plans her ways, but the Lord directs her steps* **Proverbs 16:9.**

While waiting on the Lord, I have continued to experience ongoing training through fellowship with the Holy Spirit. However, before I proceed, let me warn that there are perquisites to ongoing communion with the Holy Spirit. He is pure and righteous and I had to purpose to stay pure, guarding my heart for this relationship to grow deeper. As an appointed vessel I had to stay clean. This cleansing came by the revelation of the Holy Spirit, convicting and showing what I needed to address or renounce to maintain the purity of the vessel. All aspects of the flesh must die in order to experience the fullness of the Holy Spirit. Spirit begets Spirit, flesh begets flesh. *Walk in the Spirit and you shall not fulfill the desires of the flesh* **Galatians 5:16.**

I have also experienced different levels of deliverances and exposures to things I needed to renounce. I've come to learn that since God is holy and He desires to dwell in fellowship with us, He purifies the temples that He wants to dwell in. This purification is an ongoing process and He does so depending on the level of spiritual maturity that we are in. For example around July 2015, I received revelation regarding self-imposed beliefs that I had developed to strongholds. Most of the false beliefs were based past negative experiences; so I unknowingly formed negative opinions and attitudes about myself, others and situations. What God showed me is that once these negative mindsets and false beliefs are recognized, and renounced, deliverance becomes easy and quick without fear of having a revolving cycle around the same issues. The Holy Spirit then revealed the false beliefs I needed to renounce in different areas in my life and the deliverance became so easy and I received total freedom. Remember God had started working on me in 2009 when I became fully committed to Him. So asked I God, why He did not show me this in 2009 and when you are being delivered from other things. The answer was simple, I needed to be spiritually mature to understand what He required and to receive spiritual understanding of what was going on. I also learned from the Holy Spirit that deliverance comes much easier when you have an understanding of the root or stronghold of what you need deliverance from.

§ The Holy Spirit operates in themes or Seasons.
Do not fight the season or the direction the Holy Spirit is talking you.
First being the True Holy Spirit, He will not lead you astray.
Second, when you align and cooperate with Him
The Holy Spirit does much more when He is in control§

Revelations, insights and visitations also increased in this season depending on what the Holy Spirit wants to teach or show you. Personally, the details of my calling were revealed in such seasons, leading me on a specific path of what I needed to study and learn more about. The training of the Holy Spirit is ongoing depending on what He wants you to learn in that season. So I would encourage you to write down or journal every experience and most importantly pray about them. Ask the Holy Spirit to explain what you do not understand, where needed, seek direction from a mentor or pastor. I must warn that all of these came still with seasons of prayer and fasting. When we have genuine hunger for God, He responds by filling us. My prayer then, and continues to be for *"God to fill me with your fullness, the fullness of Christ and the fullness of the Holy Spirit".*

In this journey, I have also discovered the need, urgency and importance of constantly guarding our hearts and putting on the breastplate of righteousness. These I believe are part of the ongoing purification process of this journey. The mouth only speaks out of the abundance of the heart, *Watch over your heart with all diligence because from it springs issues of life whether good or evil.* **Proverbs 4:23.** What is in the heart is acquired by what we eat. Eating can be defined as what we entertain, absorb, tolerate and spend time in. If we spend time in the flesh or ungodly things, that gets deposited in the heart. If we spend time in the things of the Spirit, the heart receives the fullness of the Spirit and hence it speaks. So it's imperative that we guard what goes into the heart and where the Holy Spirit dwells.

The breastplate protects the heart. *I Thessalonians 5:8* defines the breastplate of righteousness as walking in "faith and love." We must walk in the faith that God who has called us and trust Him fully in this training season; this means total trust in God. In addition to the definitions of love in *I Corinthians 13,* in ministry, love calls for humility, lowliness, gentleness, patience, longsuffering, showing love by being tolerant of others and endeavoring (doing our best) to keep unity of the spirit by cultivating peace in our relationships according to *Ephesians 4; 1-4* and as directed by the Holy Spirit. We are to accept everything by faith and apply or minister to others in love. Doing this lends no effort to being flesh driven but Christ focused as He also gave in love trusting in God the Father to deliver what God had promised.

In order to receive the fullness of God, the order of His kingdom is; righteousness, peace, then joy in the Holy Spirit. The order or sequence does not change, it first starts with righteousness. This righteousness first comes through salvation by the atoning blood of Jesus Christ. Once received by Christ, this righteousness is sustained by putting on the breastplate faith. Why? Because the just (righteous) shall live by faith, *Habakkuk 2.4, Romans, 1:17, Galatians 3:11 and Hebrews10:38*, and because without faith no one can please *Hebrews 11:6*. Faith and love are inseparable, they must coexist and applied simultaneously for effective ministry. So the other needed aspect of the breastplate is love. Then we must also put on the love for without love all is vain *ICorinthians 13:1*. So note that faith and love must be applied concurrently; you cannot apply the faith and leave love out or apply love and neglect faith.

In my journey so far, I am beginning to learn that the Holy Spirit teaches in themes. These are the seasons of the Holy Spirit. He may start by an indication on an area you need to study or deal with and only progress to show or teach you more after you understand what He previously assigned to teach or address with you. So be sensitive to the themes of His operations and cooperate with Him. When you cooperate with the Holy Spirit, He flows freely and also shows you more or does more with you. Key point also is not to fight the Holy Spirit when He directs the area you need to focus. This also applies to prayer. When submitted to the Holy Spirit in prayer, let Him take the lead, do not force what is in your mind to pray, let the Holy Spirit control your tongue and mind during prayer. A lot happens supernaturally when the Spirit is in control. Do not insist of earning something different when the Spirit is directing you to learn something else. From personal experience, the Holy Spirit starts by identifying areas that need purging, cleansing or deliverance. Recently (fall, 2015) during a period of prayer and fasting, the first area that the Holy Spirit led me to renounce and repent of was flesh; carnality. However, these were not the generally known aspects of the flesh, they are the inner things that I generally would not think of. Mostly the Spirit dealt with me concerning my mindset and religious beliefs, intentions and desires in ministry and self-reliance in ministry. He taught me potential areas to trap the familiarity with the things of God and by reading Ephesians through Timothy repeatedly, the Spirit taught me more concerning requirements and characteristics of those called to ministry who will stand to the end. Once clean, He fills you more with Him then extends to show you other things He wants you to learn or know. This almost looks like *"the preparation of the vessel (you) to receive more"*. That's the best way I can explain it, hope you get the point.

§ *That when God directs or imparts, usually it is for an impending assignment. God does not just fill for fillings-sake. He imparts, anoints and fills for a task*§

Another example from personal experience; this summer I had purposed to set aside reading other material and focus on reading the Bible more. My goal was by the Holy Spirit, to understand and be filled with the Word of God. So I indulged in reading the Bible, studying and taking notes at the revelation of the Holy Spirit. With every Book of the Bible that I read, I learned something new, and most scriptures turned to intercessory prayer areas for souls, nations, families and myself. Then for a long season, I was led to read the entire Book of Psalms read repeatedly almost over three months. The previous year, I was led to read the Book of Hebrews repeatedly. After these experiences, new things were birthed in me .So I am learning to flow with the Holy Spirit but most importantly paying close attention to why He is leading in a certain direction. When this happens, my approach is now *"Lord open my eyes to see what you are teaching me and where to apply the teaching.*" My mentor taught me that when God directs or imparts, usually it is for an impending assignment. God does not just fill for fillings-sake. He imparts, anoints and fills for a task. So receive but also ask the Holy Spirit to open your eyes to know the timing of that assignment; to discern whom you are assigned to minister to. When that time comes, apply or exercise what the Spirit taught or showed you.

Finally, among the many lessons that I continue to learn throughout the journey in the Holy Spirit is that this journey requires constant submission to the Holy Spirit and rededication to the Lord. By totally submitting to the Holy Spirit, we experience the fullness of the Holy Spirit as well as being open to any direction from Him. When we see His sovereignty, it brings us back to God to rededicate everything to HIM.

*****

Pause for Action

I am a fan of the Holy Spirit; a fanatic indeed! In fact, from the time I became born again at the age of 12, the two areas in the Christian walk that I have remained attached and excited about are; prayer and the Holy Spirit. These areas draw me like a magnet! Like a little girl in a candy store, excited jumping around on a sugar high! That is exactly what prayer and the Holy Spirit make me feel. I draw a deeper attraction. This is why I encourage you to enjoy your time with the Holy Spirit. He is very personable; He has a sense of humor and yet can be firm, He directs calmly, yet can also admonish strongly. He is all knowing, when He reveals Himself in power, He is amazing yet He can still sit with you at lunch or dinner, comfort you and have one on one debate. His debates normally lead to a deeper revelation about God; leaving me in prostrate worship most of the time. The one time deliverer, counsel, defense and comforter; the Person or the Holy Spirit.

- ♦ Seriously, enjoy your time with Him even when He chastens, it is always for the best. Love applied in just a different way.
- ♦ Do not resist His flow, cooperate with what He is teaching you in that season.
- ♦ Do not rush to enter someone else's season, stay in your own.

- He leads in various paths, some long some short, adjust yourself for the path He is taking you on. Become complacent and ready to do a fast track or a long distance course in this journey.
- Write down what He teaches or shows you and pray over them. You are likely to use these in the future.
- Understand and purpose to walk in the perquisites of the Holy Spirit, righteousness, holiness, faith love, peace and joy in the Holy Spirit.
- Purpose to know this wonderful Person of the Holy Spirit by spending more time with Him in prayer. Pray more in the Spirit. Let Him get to know you and minster to you.
- Submit to the Holy Spirit in prayer. Let your prayers be Holy Spirit led, not you led or being led by your understanding or mind. He does much more when He is in control! Hallelujah to the Lamb of God!
- Walk in the Spirit and stay constantly in the Spirit and you will not fulfill the desires of the flesh.
- Be Holy Spirit Filled and Holy Spirit Led.

§

BOOK-V
CONCLUSION

§

CAREER OR VOCATION APPLICATION

§§

Scripture: *Every good gift and perfect gift is from above and comes down from Father of lights, with whom there is no variation or shadow of turning.*
James 1:17

As believers, we are ministers in whatever area we are in. Whether at home, office, market place, business, dining out, in social media, social and family interaction; we are ministers and are ministering whether we know it or not. Ministry like salvation is a lifestyle that is not limited to the pulpit! Therefore, understand that you are ministering where you are.

Secondly every gift is from above and is given uniquely tailored to what God wants you to accomplish on earth. Even though we may have similar careers, God may have still called you to accomplish specific assignments individually and not like others. So career gifts and vocations are also assigned by God for a specific assignment to bring Him glory. It is thus crucial that you ask God for your vocation and walk into the career He has designed for you. Do not launch into any career with false or wrong motives or because others are pursuing the same career. You will end up unfulfilled in your vocation. Simply ask God for what you need. Growing up, I always wanted to study law and become a judge. However, later in life at the revelation of the Holy Spirit, it became clear that my strongest skills are administration and this was later confirmed prophetically in 2014 a month after I joined a new church in West Chester, PA.

However; also looking back from age 14, I always saw myself as an executive dressed in a suit in a high level executive position. The more I reflect on this, the more I have now seen how the administrative and leadership skills tie with the actual ministerial call that God has assigned. I still gained exposure to law but God's main call for me was in administrative leadership. So I encourage you to ask God then pursue only what He wants you to do. *We have different gifts according to the grace given unto us, let us use them. If prophesy, let us prophesy in proportion to our faith; if teaching, then teach; if to encourage then encourage; if it's to give, then give generously, if it is to lead, do it ravenously, if it is show mercy, show mercy with cheerfulness,* **Romans 12:6-8** So stick to the gift and career God gave you.

Moreover, comparing yourself with others makes you susceptible to what I term "vagabond spirit". This spirit manifests as a wandering spirit always wasting a lot of time pursuing endless careers or businesses that fail to come to maturity. One may jump from one career to the next, one degree to the other without actually ever mastering and advancing professionally.

God created each of us with specific gifts to serve Him. We serve God when we serve people assigned to us. So a career or vocation is a service to God and should be done in a way that honors God. *Each of you should use whatever gift you have received to serve others, as faithful stewards of God's grace in various forms.* **1 Peter 4;10.** Our Service is unto God not man.

****

Pause for Action

As you evaluate your current career or position in the market place, the most critical question you should ask is whether you are in the career that God designed for you. If you are, the next question is whether you are maximizing your full potential by enhancing your skills to show yourself approved. Biblical principles and the counsel of the Holy Spirit should still serve as foundations for growth in your profession. As you ponder on the questions above, I would also recommend the following:

- ◆ Realize that you are the Child of God; born again and a representation of Christ in the work place.
- ◆ Recognize that you are employed to serve and honor God.
- ◆ As the child of God, through prayer, take authority over the environment and territory or city you are working in by the Blood of Jesus and in the Name of Jesus.
- ◆ Establish the kingdom of God in your work environment and office.

- Tithe your earnings and save a percentage of your money. Crown Financial Ministries by Dave Ramsey. Maintain good financial guides from budgeting to a money map for debt free living. Avoid debt.
- Respect, honor and serve all in your work place.
- Adhere to your employer's policies and procedures; avoid short cuts.
- Represent God in your dress code and personal appearance. I am a strong believer in "first impressions."
- Show interest in the employer and take opportunities to develop your skills within the organization. Enroll in mentorship or career development programs.
- Where certifications are required, obtain necessary job related certifications. Doing this gives you the upper edge for future promotions or compensation.
- Through the guidance of the Holy Spirit, seize promotional opportunities that arise, do not be afraid to try something new. Take calculated risks.
- Separate yourself. Associate with achievers, and peers in higher positions than you are. Doing this will expose you to new things or knowledge.
- Choose your friends wisely; interact with those who enhance and develop you positively.
- Seek counsel from God. Humans can knowingly give you wrong counsel.
- Avoid work place relationships that can compromise your development in the work place.
- Beware of the competitive destructive spirits; pray frequently for your job.
- Maintain moral standards at work. Great men and women have lost their careers due to downfalls related to moral and ethical standards. Walk in the Spirit and you shall fulfill the desires of the flesh.
- Do your best in the work place. I learned this from Dr. Creflo Dollar, and watch God reward and promote you.
- Be sure to develop a transitional plan should you decide to leave work to pursue ministry. First ensure and confirm that living work is God's directive. Save money and plan your "financial exit plan". Unless absolutely sure, never leave a job abruptly to pursue business or ministry without a plan.

♦ It is best advised that you look for another job while still working in your present position. Never quit voluntarily without a contingency plan.

♦ Stop switching jobs abruptly. Job histories are reviewed as part of the employment process. The duration you stay in a position is commonly scrutinized. Your commitment to an employer can be evaluated based on the duration you have worked. "Job hoppers" are a deterrent to employers. Likewise, "church hoppers'" would be a concern to pastors.

♦ Serve unto God not man. Honor God with all your substance.

CONCLUSION

§§

Scripture: *-Do you not know that those who run in a race all run, but one receives the prize? Run in such a way that you may obtain it.* **I Corinthians 9:24**

In summary, the entire book is somehow a journal of my ongoing journey in ministry but should also serve as guide to any area of vocation in life as designed by God's will. I have prayed that this book provides guidance and illuminates areas in your calling and serves as a catalyst; activating and causing every reader to take action and start walking towards what God assigned them. Let's review each chapter to refresh our minds:

Introduction to Ministry-Evaluate your life and identify Spiritual gifts that you tend to experience frequently and are drawn to. You operate in these gifts with ease and less effort and or you have fellowship and visitations of the Holy Spirit and are able to discern God's voice. These serve as possible hints that you have calling or gifts that require development.

Can Natural Gifts be used in Ministry- Evaluate natural gifts (career or professional) that you have. Do you find yourself naturally responding and taking on the same roles outside your work setting? Your professional roles may be utilized in church, ministries or fellowship. For instance, if you are a supervisor at work, you may be assigned to oversee a department or project at your church. People may just vote or pick you to lead them in projects. Since God is the giver of all gifts; both spiritual and natural gifts are crucial and will be utilized in the assignment God has for you. *Whatever you do, in word or indeed, do all in the name of the Lord Jesus, giving thanks to God the Father through Him,* **Colossians 3:17.**

The Journey Begins-God draws us to His attention in various ways. To some though actual encounters with God through angelic or visitations, dreams and vision. To others through speech; the audible voice of God that they would hear and respond to. Finally to some, "an experience or situation that will cause you to seek God". This latter way, is how my journey started. Either way, the most important thing is not to resist the call. Submit and surrender totally to God.

The Shredding- I consider this period as a period of separation and purging. I have defined it as a season which feels like the peeling of an onion. Layer by layer God sequentially prunes and chastens removing what is unholy, the dying of the flesh from outer core then inner core. This is an ongoing process and can be done in stages of maturity through God. I believe God does the shredding at His timing also; waiting until having being matured to gain understanding of what is being pruned and the reason it should prune you. Interestingly, this chastening process usually occurs when you least expect it. In fact, when you think you have covered all bases, in right standing with God; then He shows you another layer that you need to peel off. Embrace the shredding, pruning, the chastening; it is God's love for us exemplified to make us a reflection of Him. God is holy, we therefore must be holy. It is transformation to His image and finally the pruning allows for more productivity, fresh oil and new impartation for greater works! Embrace this process and do not resist.

Committing to the Call- This is the most critical part of this journey, your commitment to the call. It should be noted that this commitment though made initially while accepting the Call, is also an ongoing daily and lifetime commitment to God. It is a commitment that presses through good and bad days, adversity, life and ministry pressures, emotions and hurts, feelings and people, life or death. Commitment involves taking the risk, counting the cost, serving out of a pure heart with Christ centered intentions and most important, commitment out of your love for God.

The Ministry of the Holy Spirit, the Personal Trainer- It is imperative that we submit to the Holy Spirit because the initial and ongoing training in ministry begins and ends with the Holy Spirit. Therefore, it is just as crucial that there is nothing including a man or a woman who can substitute the training of the Holy Spirit for you. It is important that we fellowship with Him regularly, die of the flesh and walk in the Spirit in order to synchronize and be in harmony with the Holy Spirit. John Paul Jackson teaches that in the training phase, the Holy Spirit trains in the things of the Spirit first, then character, then doctrine. This was the exact sequence of my journey and continues to be. However, your role is to submit to Holy Spirit in whatever area He wants to train you on. I'm warning you submit, lest you repeat the same lessons over and over. In this training also, it is the Holy Spirit who determines the course outline, its intensity and whether you have passed or need to retake the training. I am warning you again, do not, ever try to dictate the Holy Spirit. God chose you for the call, you did not choose you!

Seek Mentorship at the Direction of the Holy Spirit- I would like to reiterate here that once submitted to God, everything moving forward must be at the direction of the Holy Spirit. You must strive to cultivate your relationship with the Holy Spirit and His voice or how He communicates with you. This is important because of the increase of deceptive voices which divert God's plan for you by leading you to the wrong mentor. You do not want to be under a false mentor whose source of authority you do not know! That said, the Holy Spirit will determine and appoint the type of mentorship you need. This may translate to either attending a Bible school, joining a ministry or church or submitting to a pastor. Once confirmed, it is now up to you to submit to your mentor. Purpose to learn as much as you can under the mentor. The key issues here are; submission, humility and diligence.

Mentor- Mentee Relationship-It is important to keep being reminded that you are under the direction of the Holy Spirit and the mentors have been appointed by God for you. Therefore, honor them as God's servants and not friends or peers. Professional and ministerial boundaries must be set at the very start of the mentorship relationship. Your mentor is not your friend and you should not consider him/her causally. Respect others your mentor may assign to you and don't relate to them with the same expectations you have of your mentor. Inquire from your mentor how he or she would like to be accessed. Accessibility is important not only for learning but for obtaining feedback in evaluating progress and outlining future goals. Show interest in the mentorship process and seek your mentor in order to learn more.

Transitioning-Ending the Mentorship Relationship- Consider the following as a guideline for ending the mentorship relationship, or ending the relationship with any ministry or department you have been serving; be sure with confirmation from the Holy Spirit and or from your mentor that your assignment is over, review the terms and goals of the mentorship and ensure all objectives have been met, set time to meet with your mentor to review the mentorship objectives and discuss the transition plans, provide updates of assignments or projects you were assigned to ensure the mentor can reassign them, formally thank your mentor for the mentorship preferably through face to face meeting, if unable write a formal letter, do not leave unexpectedly. If you must leave, give advance notice, preferably a month, maintain professionalism and respect in your communication and interaction in your final meetings. This is key even when you have differences in opinion. Agree to disagree respectfully. Do not slander your mentor, ministry or department even if you know they were at fault or you know their weaknesses. Leave the doors of communication open and end your mentorship with mutual respect for each other.

Lessons from Mentorship Experiences- I would recommend writing down or journaling every lesson learned for future reference. Where applicable, put into practice immediately what you have learned. Practice makes perfect, so develop the newly acquired lesson through continuous practical application. Also note that although self-programmed to learn one thing, God may expose you to others areas that He may want you to learn during your mentorship program. Therefore, be discerning, flexible and open to those areas. Consider them just as important as knowing God is not partial, I believe He provides comprehensively having already seen the end from the beginning.

Personal Responsibility- Ninety nine percent (99%) of this journey in ministry is done in the private and solitude training of the Holy Spirit. Mentorship only compliments and provides practical setting for application of what was taught. This calls for evaluation of our intent or reason for pursuing the Call, followed by independent intentionally seeking of God through prayer. I believe that God desires that we experience Him independently first before we share that experience to others. Secondly, there are just some things God wants to reveal to us alone and to distinctly know His voice and ways. Collectively, all these lead us to knowing God for ourselves! To rely on a mentor to hear from God for you is idolatry and also puts you at a risk for exposure to divination, sorcery and false prophesies. Learn to now God for yourself by committing to prayer, fasting, reading the Bible, meditating on the Word of God, walking in the Holy Spirit, renewing our mind with the Word of God, and being Holy Spirit filled and Holy Spirit led.

Rejection, Offense and Mockery-When God allows us to experience any type of adversity while on this journey, I believe the adversaries are mostly meant for our good even when we don't understand them. Because God desires that we experience His fullness and be transformed to His image, He uses tests such as rejection, offense and mockery to shape our character to His. On the contrary, these tests can also be demonically inspired and most attacks will come from your inner circle of immediate friends, believers and family. Regardless of their sources, be sure to stay focused on the assignment God has called you for. Discern each situation and ask the Holy Spirit to help you identify what He is trying to teach, as he grooms or matures you. Most important, do not lose your anointing over an offense.

Seek God not the Gifts- God is the one who calls and chooses for ministry, we do not call ourselves. Since God called us, He knows the gifts that are necessary and appropriate to accomplish our assignments. Therefore, do not loath after anyone's gift or imitate someone. Coveting another's gift has the risky potential of opening doors to demonic gift! Simply related to God. Communicate and have fellowship with Him. Ask God to equip you with the gifts necessary to accomplish His will in the assignment He has assigned to you. This asking or seeking, comes through purposed consistent time with God in prayer, reading the Bible, meditation of His Word and fasting. Seek first the Kingdom of God and everything else shall be added.

Do not rush or fight for the pulpit or microphone- The one thing I learned by revelation was that the pulpit is a very dangerous place. One must be fully prepared and equipped for the pulpit and microphone, one because of the accountability level that God holds you for His flock, second; because of the spiritual warfare associated with this. Do not promote yourself in ministry; God chose you, let Him promote. The other advice is that do not launch out prematurely. Denounce and submit every anxiety and individuals who would want to push you out prematurely. Instead, perfect and excel in every assigned duty you have been given in your mentorship or auxiliary until the appointed time comes. Refrain from appointing yourself titles; those who God has assigned to officiate you will give you the appropriate title. Finally, before you launch out, it is important to be officially prayed for, blessed, anointed and activated in your calling by those God has placed in spiritual authority over you. This time too will be determined and the ordination process orchestrated by God. The Holy Spirit will tell you when you are ready to launch out. God will open the right doors and platforms for your ministry. Relax!

Enjoy your seasons with the Holy Spirit- I love the Holy Spirit as my best friend, companion and the ultimate teacher! Enjoy your seasons with Him. Spend more time in prayer; praying more in tongues. Journal everything He tells you and apply the lesson practically. Expect greater things with the Holy Spirit but also note that obedience, love, holiness, faith and guarding your heart are crucial for a successful, intimate and maturing relationship with the Holy Spirit. The fullness of the Holy Spirit can only be experienced by total submission to Him.

Career or Vocation Application- All gifts and skills have been given to us by God. We should pursue the careers and vocations God appointed for us instead of pursuing what others do. We must represent Christ and establish His kingdom in the work place. Prayer and guidance of the Holy Spirit are paramount foundations that must be laid and constantly sorted in our jobs. Take advantage of career development opportunities that are offered by your supervisors. Be bold and take calculated risks. Work as serving God. Tithe and save money. Work in order to eat. Serve and honor God with all your substance.

I trust that by reading this book you have found clarification in different aspects of your journey with the Lord. As relayed in the introductory chapter, information shared in this book can be applied to any areas of vocation whether in ministry, career or business. I frequently read the entire Bible from Genesis to Revelation and each time I am amazed to learn that truly the principles, guidelines and solution to every issue and area in life is in the Bible. That is why the foundational guide in this book applies to all aspects of life.

Ministry is not limited to the pulpit. Let us therefore be mindful that like the servants who were given, 10 and 100 talents (scripture), we will give account of how we utilized the talents. As those called, now let us run in such a way that we may obtain the crown, being confident of this one thing, that He who began a good work in us, will complete it until the day of Jesus Christ. Amen.

Blessings.

PRAYER OF COMMITMENT OR RECOMMENTMENT TO MINISTRY

§§

Scripture: Isaiah 42:3-7 *A bruised reed He will not break, and smoking flax He will not quench;*

*He will bring forth justice for truth. He will not fail nor be discouraged. Till He has established justice in the earth; and the coastlands shall wait for His law. "Thus says God the Lord, Who created the heavens and stretched them out, Who spread forth the earth and that which comes from it, Who gives breath to the people on it, And spirit to those who walk on it: "**I, the Lord, have called You in righteousness, And will hold Your hand; I will keep You and give You as a covenant to the people**, As a light to the Gentiles, To open blind eyes, To bring out prisoners from the prison, Those who sit in darkness from the prison house.*

If you sense that you derailed in your journey in ministry and want to recommit to the Lord who called you, read the above scripture. God will not break or quench what He birthed in you. Pray the following.

Father in the name of Jesus, I come to you as your son or daughter. I submit to your Lordship and repent of my sins. (If you know the specific areas, please name the areas. For example, I repent for rebelling or for the bitterness that led me to leave ministry). I renounce this sin (s) and for your forgiveness. I repent of any consequences my actions may have caused the Body of Christ, my church, family, friends, pastors or mentors. I appropriate the Blood of Jesus to cleanse me of my sins and receive Jesus Christ as my Lord and Savior. I ask the Holy Spirit to fill me anew. I submit to you Holy Spirit; guide me in knowledge, wisdom, revelation, and discernment and counsel to walk and accomplish the assignment God has for me. Holy Spirit, fill me with your gifts that I may experience the fullness of God in this new life and complete my assignment in the name of Jesus. Amen! Thank you Lord that I am now in right standing with you; Holy Spirit take over from now.

After completing this prayer, review the summarized key points in the Conclusion Chapter of this book. I've prayed that God will lead you to the right assembly of believers, church or fellowship for successful mentorship as you resume fellowship with the Holy Spirit and do your part in God's Kingdom.

Welcome, I've got your back! We are in this together, it is all about ONE Kingdom!

CALL TO SALVATION & FILLING
OF THE HOLY SPIRIT

§§

Scripture (s) John 14:6-7. *Jesus said to him, "I am the way, the truth, and the life. No one comes to the Father except through Me. If you had known Me, you would have known My Father also; and from now on you know Him and have seen Him.*

I John 1:8-9- *If we say that we have no sin, we deceive ourselves, and the truth is not in us. If we confess our sins, God is faithful and just to forgive us our sins and to cleanse us from all unrighteousness.*

Maybe you are at your wits end and you just want God to reach out to you and realign you to the marvelous plan He has for you. Invite Him to come in and take the lead by saying this prayer:

Dear God, I come to you. I accept your Son Jesus Christ as my Lord and Savior. I believe that Jesus died and rose again for my sins that I may receive salvation. I therefore repent of my sins and ask for your forgiveness. I renounce sin. Lord Jesus now come to my life both in me and in everything that concerns me. Come in Lord Jesus and be Lord over my life and align me to the path and plan you have set for me. In the name of Jesus Christ, I pray. Amen.

Now invite the Holy Spirit who will serve as your helper and guide among many things in this new life. Say, Holy Spirit, I now welcome you to reside me and take over every aspect of my life. I submit to you Holy Spirit; guide me in knowledge, wisdom, revelation, and discernment and counsel to walk and accomplish the plan God has for me. Holy Ghost, fill me with your gifts that I may experience the fullness of God in this new life, in the name of Jesus I pray. Amen! Oh beloved of the Lord, the Holy Spirit now resides in and with you. Watch out for what He is about to do!

With arms opened wide, welcome to the Kingdom of God! The next step is to look for a local church whose beliefs and doctrine align with the Word of God. I have already prayed that the Holy Spirit will connect you with the right believers who will help and guide you to maturity in Christ Jesus.

On your end, set some time at least twice a day to pray and read the Bible. Prayer is simply talking to God. Ask the Holy Spirit to teach you how to pray and then just pray. To start, pray when you first wake up and talk to God the way you talk to a friend you respected and be open to God, telling Him everything. If you can only pray 5 minutes twice a day, do that, then increase your prayer time daily. With time the Holy Spirit will mature your prayer life if you stay consistent.

You may read the Bible before or after your prayer time. Purchase a version or download a Bible app that you can easily understand such as the New Living Translation (NLT) or New International Version (NIV). I prefer the New King James Version, but occasionally, I read other versions when I need clarification. When you are about to open the Bible, ask the Holy Spirit to illuminate and bring clarity to what you are about to read. The Holy Spirit is very good at this. This is His job; our helper, He reveals the truth to us. Start by reading the book of Proverbs and the Gospel of John. You can read one chapter of Proverbs when you wake up and a chapter from John before bedtime. Purpose to memorize a scripture a day and meditate on the scripture that caught your attention. With time, the Word of God will become alive in your heart and in your thoughts. Before you know it, you would have read the entire Bible. When you get there start anew. By the help of the Holy Spirit this is how we grow; it takes personal responsibility.

I am so proud of you. I've got your back too. I am praying for you!

OTHER BOOKS BY THE AUTHOR

§§

The Alternative Plan

*Released in the summer of 2015, this book is written to young professionals in the work place as well as young adults from high school to those just launching into their first careers; to assure then that **God can still realign your life to fit the plan He intended for you**. This book is written to those questioning their future, it ministers to the wounded and those seeking security in their lives. Self-reliance or independence is one of the areas Satan uses to sabotage the plan of God for you. The book highlights God's ability to clean up and restore to fullness, even the greatest mess. Through reading this book, may you receive salvation, healing, deliverance, restoration and restitution in the Name of Jesus through His Blood! The purpose of this book is to bring hope to the reader and provide direction on how to get back to the plan God intended for you.*

ISBN-978-0-9898247-6-7. Hardcover. 55 pages

For copies contact Pauline at belovedpolly@gmail.com or available on Kindle or from Amazon.com

CONTACT INFORMATION & FOR SPEAKING ENGAGEMENTS

§§

Pauline Adongo
The Ministry of Jesus Christ International
P.O Box 2572
West Chester, PA 19380
Email:belovedpolly@gmail.com

Printed in the United States
By Bookmasters